THE QUIET REVOLUTION

The Struggle for the Rights of Disabled Americans

Also by James Haskins

THE CREOLES OF COLOR OF NEW ORLEANS

Through their activism, the disabled have won several landmark victories in the courts and important legislation on both the state and federal levels. (The President's Committee on Employment of the Handicapped)

THE QUIET REVOLUTION

The Struggle for the Rights
of Disabled Americans

by James Haskins
with J M Stifle

A JOHN DAY BOOK

Thomas Y. Crowell   New York

8 19

Grateful acknowledgment is made to the following for permission to reprint material copyrighted or controlled by them:

Random House, Inc., for quotation from *W. H. Auden: Collected Poems.* Edited by Edward Mendelson. Copyright 1940, renewed 1968 by W. H. Auden. Reprinted by permission of Random House, Inc.

Leonard Kriegel for excerpt from "Uncle Tom and Tiny Tim: Some Reflections on the Cripple as Negro," from *The American Scholar,* vol. 38, no. 3 (Summer 1969). Reprinted by permission of Leonard Kriegel.

Random House, Inc., for excerpts from *Willowbrook: A Report on How It Is and Why It Doesn't Have to Be That Way.* Copyright © 1972 by Geraldo Rivera. Reprinted by permission of Random House, Inc.

Designed by Kim Llewellyn

LIBRARY OF CONGRESS CATALOGING IN PUBLICATION DATA
Haskins, James, 1941–
The quiet revolution.
Bibliography.
Includes index.
SUMMARY: Focuses on the human and civil rights the handicapped are campaigning for, and on the various methods they are using to bring change to society and make it more aware of the needs of the disabled.
1. Physically handicapped—Civil rights—United States—Juvenile literature. [1. Physically handicapped—Civil rights] I. Stifle, J. M., joint author. II. Title.
HV3023.A3H37 1979   362.4′0973   77–27664
ISBN 0–690–03981–6
ISBN 0–690–03982–4 lib. bdg.

First Edition

*Dreamed I saw a building
with a thousand floors
A thousand windows and a
thousand doors
Not one of them was ours
my dear
Not one of them was ours*
—W. H. AUDEN

CONTENTS

THE QUIET REVOLUTION

The Struggle for the Rights of Disabled Americans

INTRODUCTION

The Constitution is the fundamental law of the land and the rights outlined in it are guaranteed to all American citizens. For some persons, though, the law is there to be broken, and the rights of others ignored when such rights interfere with their own selfish interests. Our country has grown up with a double standard in human and civil rights that has allowed the African slave trade, intolerance of certain religious beliefs and ethnic groups, persecution of those with opposing political views, exploitation of child labor, and suppression of women.

The Founding Fathers did, however, provide oppressed persons with a means of securing the protection of their rights in the form of the judiciary and legislative branches of our government. But seeking the restoration of one's rights through the courts or the legislature can be a lengthy, expensive, and often fruitless process. It is customary in this country for individuals who share a particular grievance to band together in order to fight more effectively for their common cause. Throughout its history, America has witnessed the formation of many such special-interest groups, ranging from political parties, abolitionists, organized labor, female suffragists, to black civil-rights activists, antiwar demonstrators, down to the current women's equal-rights advocates.

A number of very effective techniques for drawing attention and support to a cause have come out of these different movements. The list includes civil disobedience, the strike, the protest demonstration, and the boycott. (At times, some groups have even used violence to dramatize their grievances.) With their unity and the strength of their numbers on behalf of a cause, these special interest groups have often been successful in securing their civil rights.

There is one group of American citizens, however, that has remained largely unorganized although its members have been regularly oppressed throughout our nation's history. These people have been ignored, excluded, and isolated from society and routinely denied their most basic human and legal rights. Their particular situation of forced separation from society and from one another has prevented them from joining together to fight for the improvement of their status as citizens. Because they have remained hidden from view, their plight has gone generally unnoticed. Until recently, the majority of Americans probably never even considered the possibility that this group has suffered any injustice.

This group is made up of the large number of Americans —approximately one in four—who are physically or mentally disabled in some way. They include the man in the wheelchair who is unable to vote because he cannot make it up the steps to the entrance at the polling place; the deaf child who cannot obtain an adequate education because there is no place for him in the public school system; the dwarf who cannot reach the dial on a public telephone; the one-armed man who is denied employment because he is considered an "insurance risk"; the stroke victim who is unable to receive proper treatment and rehabilitation because he doesn't live near the right facilities; and the factory worker growing progressively deaf because of the high noise levels where he works but who receives no compensation for this disability because it is not recognized as job-related. These cases are representative of a sizable group of Americans whose human and civil rights are being violated.

In the late 1960's a quiet revolution began to spread across the nation, spearheaded by disabled activists and their supporters. Disabled Americans started to come out of their pockets of isolation to band together to fight for the cause they hold in common—the elimination of the prejudice and discrimination that have prevented them from leading lives of dignity and independence. They have been presenting their case in the courts, lobbying their legislatures, and publicly demonstrating for the removal of all the physical, social, legal, and economic barriers to their enjoyment of full citizenship. This book is about the disabled and the ongoing fight for their fundamental rights.

This is a fight that has importance for all Americans. Statistics show that most Americans can expect to be disabled at least temporarily at some point during their lives. The probability of disability and the length of its duration increase with age. As the life expectancy of all Americans, including the disabled, increases, there are very few of us who will escape being touched by disability either personally or through our family or loved ones. It is important that we heed the cry of today's disabled activists because what they are demanding could improve the quality of life for us all.

BANISH

THESE
BARRIERS

National Easter Seal Society for Crippled Children and Adults, Inc.

1

Birth of the Disabled Rights Movement

Something many people forget is that it is easy for anyone to join this minority.

    —LYDIA LARSEN,
      San Francisco Utilities Commission
      (confined to a wheelchair as a result of an accident)

Early in 1950, six mothers who had met one another at the Muscular Dystrophy Clinic of New York where they had been taking their children for treatment, got together to talk about mutual problems. Like many other groups of parents with disabled children across the country, they began gathering informally to discuss shared experiences and frustrations encountered in their search for information and services. During their meetings they began to overcome their sense of isolation and to feel that if they worked together they might be able to improve conditions for their children.

Out of these early meetings sprang the Muscular Dystrophy Association of America. A number of other parent organizations and consumer associations devoted to the special interests of particular groups of the disabled had similar beginnings. They include the National Federation of the Blind, United Cerebral Palsy Associations, and the National Association for Retarded Children (later changed to Citizens). Where there were no public programs for the disabled, these groups created their own. They raised funds privately to support research, recreation programs, diagnostic centers, and vocational and rehabilitative training.

Perhaps even more important, these special-interest groups increased the visibility of the disabled and heightened public awareness regarding the true nature of physical disability. They publicized their work through news letters and other publications, direct-mail campaigns, public meetings, in the various news media, and by such events as "walka-thons" and "telethons." Their efforts helped to destigmatize disability, to make it less threatening to the general public. This, in turn, paved the way for widespread support of improved public services and, later, the movement for full citizenship for the disabled.

The black civil-rights movement of the 1960's spurred the efforts of these groups. Like blacks and other minorities, disabled Americans also suffered from prejudice, discrimination, segregation, personal degradation, and economic deprivation—all of which contributed to the denial of their basic human and legal rights. As one disabled activist put it: "Blacks were relegated to the back of the bus; we can't even get on the bus."

Many of the groups who represented the disabled began to adopt the methods and tactics used by blacks and other minority groups to secure and protect their rights. They launched letter-writing campaigns, participated in sit-ins, "wheel-ins," boycotts, and public demonstrations. They lobbied state legislatures and the United States Congress for laws that would end discrimination and improve public services. And they sued in the courts for the protection of their rights.

In the early 1970's the struggle for their rights increased in urgency as more and more of the disabled themselves became involved. They began forming activist groups of their own and speaking out for themselves, rather than relying on their parents and friends to act on their behalf. Among these groups were the National Paraplegia Foundation, Paralyzed Veterans of America, Disabled In Action, Inc., and the American Coalition of Citizens with Disability, a national coalition of disabled-activist organizations.

"These are a new breed of handicapped people," says disabled activist Eric Gentile. "There are a lot of Vietnam veterans who feel they have given their best to their country and don't like the situation they are left in. They are not used

The President's Committee on Employment of the Handicapped

to being rolled over by society. They don't have the traditional attitude of the handicapped of accepting [discrimination] and staying at home behind closed doors."

A quadraplegic lawyer sums up the growing trend, saying, "In the past the handicapped have sat back and let others speak for them. Now there is increasing militancy on the part of the handicapped themselves. We are the next minority."

Through their activism the disabled have won several landmark victories in the courts and important legislation on both the state and federal levels, their crowning achievement being the Rehabilitation Act of 1973. Section 504 of the Rehabilitation Act is patterned after the landmark Title VI of the Civil Rights Act of 1964. It states that:

No otherwise qualified handicapped individual in the United States . . . shall, solely by reason of his handicap, be excluded from participation in, be denied benefits of, or be subjected to discrimination under any program or activity receiving federal financial assistance.

This long-overdue recognition and movement toward righting centuries-old wrongs does not mark the end of the battle for the rights of the disabled. The courts may have ruled in their favor, and laws may have been enacted for their protection, but the task of seeing to it that the rulings are upheld and the laws enforced still lies ahead. Full, equal citizenship for all the disabled remains a distant goal. The real struggle has only just begun.

2

The Rights of the Disabled and What Is Being Done to Secure Them

There is no formula that can force Tiny Tim to stand on his own two crutches. But the cripple can make a start by refusing the invisibility thrust over him by the culture. He can insist on being seen.

—LEONARD KRIEGEL,
The American Scholar

In 1975 the United Nations General Assembly adopted a resolution known as the Declaration on the Rights of Disabled Persons. Here are a few excerpts from that document:

—Disabled persons have the inherent right to respect for their human dignity . . . to enjoy a decent life, as normal and full as possible.
—Disabled persons have the same civil and political rights as other human beings. . . .
—Disabled persons have the right to . . . treatment . . . and other services which will enable them to

9

develop their capabilities and skills to the maximum and will hasten the process of their social integration. . . .

—Disabled persons have the right to economic and social security and to a decent level of living. They have the right, according to their capabilities, to secure and retain employment. . . .

—Disabled persons shall be protected against all exploitation, all regulations and all treatment of a discriminatory, abusive or degrading nature.

—Disabled persons shall be able to avail themselves of qualified legal aid when such aid proves indispensable for the protection of their persons and property.

This is a fine document and it deserves attention. But it is perhaps too general and too lofty for practical application in our less than ideal world.

The United Cerebral Palsy Associations has issued a similar document that is called a Bill of Rights for the Handicapped. Just as the Bill of Rights in the United States Constitution contains ten amendments that state rights guaranteed to American citizens, this document sets forth ten provisions which outline the major civil rights sought by the disabled. They are:

—The right to prevention of disability
—The right to health services and medical care
—The right to education
—The right to training
—The right to work

—The right to an income
—The right to live where and how they choose
—The right to barrier-free public facilities
—The right to function independently
—The right to petition

The right to petition is already guaranteed in the Bill of Rights in the United States Constitution. The First Amendment states in part that "Congress shall make no law abridging . . . the right of the people . . . to petition the government for a redress of grievances." But the United Cerebral Palsy Associations decided to include it in their Bill of Rights, too, because it is one of the most essential rights for disabled Americans, a primary means of securing and protecting all other rights within our political system. According to the UCPA: "The handicapped individual has the right to petition social institutions and the courts to gain opportunities as may be enjoyed by others but denied the handicapped because of oversight, public apathy or discrimination."

In recent years the disabled have been regularly petitioning the courts in what are known as "class-action" suits. In this particular kind of legal action, one or more individuals sue another person or group of persons on behalf of a whole group or "class" of individuals. For example, a disabled student can sue his local school board for failing to provide him or her with an adequate free public education. If the suit is a class action, the court's ruling will apply to *all* disabled students under its jurisdiction, not merely the one student who made the initial petition.

11

The disabled, like all other petitioners in the courts, rely on the Constitution for legal support of their position. The constitutional amendments most often cited in litigation brought on behalf of the disabled are the Fifth and the Fourteenth Amendments. Each has a clause that states that no person shall be deprived of "life, liberty, or property without due process of law." (The Fifth Amendment's "due process" clause applies to the federal government, while the "due process" clause in the Fourteenth Amendment covers the individual states.)

Due process provides for the legal protection of the rights of the individual. It requires that the government deal with its citizens in a reasonable and fair manner. This means that no individual can be deprived of his rights without formal notification and the opportunity to protest and possibly reverse such deprivation. Due process has many applications in cases involving the disabled. For example, a disabled individual facing involuntary commitment to an institution has the right to legal counsel and the opportunity to fight that action in a court of law.

Hand in hand with the right to due process goes another right expressed in the Fourteenth Amendment, which says: "No state shall . . . deny to any person within its jurisdiction the equal protection of the laws." The "equal protection" clause guarantees the right of all citizens to equal opportunity to participate in all aspects of life in this nation.

The Fourteenth Amendment was written into law after the Civil War, and was originally intended to assure the rights of blacks to equal citizenship. Over the years the equal-protection clause has been applied to other deprived minorities, such as the disabled.

The courts have found, however, that it is not always enough merely to proclaim the rights of all Americans to equality before the law. Further positive measures have to be taken to insure that certain groups, like blacks and the disabled, who have been relegated to second-class citizenship for so long, are able finally to move up to full citizenship.

The Fourteenth Amendment, therefore, has been broadly interpreted by the courts as a call for all-out "affirmative action" to end discrimination and to raise the status of traditionally deprived minorities. This means, for example, that not only does a paraplegic have the right to equal employment opportunity but additional provisions must be made in the workplace to suit his or her special needs.

The courts alone do not have the power to insure the equality of all Americans. This fact is recognized in the Fourteenth Amendment, which states in closing: "The Congress shall have power to enforce, by appropriate legislation, the provisions of this article." Only the United States Congress and the state legislatures can enact the formal rules and regulations that guarantee the rights of the disabled and other minorities. And only the executive branches of federal and state governments have the power to enforce those laws and rules. The courts can rule in favor of the constitutional rights of groups like the disabled, but it is the legislative and executive branches of government that have the ultimate power to insure those rights. For example, the courts can decree that the mentally retarded have a right to free public education, but it is up to the federal and state legislatures to make the laws that will guarantee that right, and to the appropriate government agencies to see that these laws are properly enforced.

Most federal legislation relating to the rights of the handicapped, such as the Rehabilitation Act of 1973, affects the dispersal of public funds. Under this type of law the federal government declares its intention to withhold financial support to any organization or institution that is not accessible to the disabled. This includes schools, hospitals, housing, transportation, welfare programs, and even private industry. Since today there are few areas of American life that do not receive some kind of federal financial aid, the federal government should be able to use this leverage to bring down the remaining obstacles to the full participation of disabled Americans in the mainstream of our nation's life. But, although such laws have been passed, they often go unenforced by the government agencies assigned to carry them out.

This kind of chronic inaction on the part of government agencies has led to a renewed feeling of frustration among disabled activists. They have fought long and hard in the courts, in Congress, and in their state legislatures, and they have won certain guarantees—on paper, at least—to their rights. These guarantees are worthless, however, if no one is willing to take the responsibility to see to it that they are properly enforced.

On April 6, 1977, groups of angry disabled citizens occupied the offices of the Department of Health, Education, and Welfare (HEW) in Washington, D.C., and several other regional locations throughout the country. The Department of

A group of citizens rallies in front of the White House in April 1977, protesting the failure of the Department of Health, Education, and Welfare to give final approval to regulations enforcing Section 504 of the Rehabilitation Act of 1973. (The President's Committee on Employment of the Handicapped)

Health, Education, and Welfare is the federal agency responsible for implementing Section 504 of the Rehabilitation Act of 1973. The disabled had gathered to protest the fact that four years had passed since the Rehabilitation Act had become law and HEW had as yet to give final approval to regulations that would enforce Section 504. As one participant in the demonstrations put it:

> The Department's failure to issue regulations has meant that hundreds of thousands of intended beneficiaries of HEW-funded programs throughout the country who are handicapped continue to be subjected to discrimination in employment, health and social services, education and access to programs.

Twenty-two days after the sit-ins began, Secretary of Health, Education, and Welfare Joseph Califano signed the new regulations into law, saying that the Rehabilitation Act "will usher in a new era of equality for handicapped individuals in which unfair barriers to self-sufficiency and decent treatment will begin to fall before the force of law."

The disabled are already questioning the range and vagueness of parts of the regulations, and what looks like their unenforceability. As Dusty Irvine, one of the leaders of the protest, said, "To have the regulations signed doesn't mean the world will miraculously change. This is just the first step."

3

The Right to Prevention
of Disability

*The handicapped individual has the right to prevention of
disability insofar as possible through early detection of abnormalities in infancy, immediate and continuous family guidance, and comprehensive habilitative services until maximum
potential is achieved.*

—A BILL OF RIGHTS FOR THE HANDICAPPED,
United Cerebral Palsy Associations

It has been estimated that between one third and one half of
all disabilities are preventable. Medical science has developed the knowledge and the techniques necessary to prevent
a great number of disabling conditions, and it has the potential to uncover ways of preventing a great many more in the
future.

Among the major causes of early permanent physical
disabilities are birth defects that are the result of genetic
abnormalities; prenatal damage to the fetus brought on by
disease, accident, or the absorption of poisonous substances;

or injury at the time of birth. Such birth-related disorders include cerebral palsy, blindness, deafness, mental retardation, and missing limbs. Many of these abnormalities can be prevented through available medical treatment if potential disorders are detected early enough in the unborn or newborn child. For example, certain kinds of congenital (existing at birth, but not hereditary) hearing loss can be lessened by prompt medical attention, and many of the disabling effects of mental retardation can be prevented or relieved by early developmental stimulation.

The many techniques and practices now known to aid the detection and prevention of disabling disorders in the infant include genetic counseling for both parents; proper nutrition; immunization against rubella (German measles) and other diseases known to cause birth defects; medical care throughout pregnancy that could uncover unsuspected diseases in the mother; and avoidance of exposure of the pregnant mother to poisonous substances such as lead, mercury, radiation, and toxic drugs.

If so much is already known about the prevention of infant disabilities, then why do so many children continue to suffer from them? The answer is that prenatal and child health-care services remain unavailable to large segments of the population, primarily those in low-income urban and rural settings.

The historic emphasis of health care in this country has been on the treatment and cure of disorders once they have occurred rather than on their initial prevention. Our total national health bill is currently estimated by the Department of Health, Education, and Welfare to run about $200 billion a year—more than 90 percent of it going for cure, while less than 3 percent goes for prevention and less than 1 percent for health education. One reason for this situation was given in a 1974 report prepared for the Department of Health, Education, and Welfare. It said:

> One [explanation] may be undervaluation of investment in prevention. In being penny-wise by conserving today's prevention funds, present-oriented policy-makers may be pound-foolish with respect to the future, considering the high human and economic costs of the handicapped person over the years.

Several studies conducted in recent years bear out this statement. One study, done in 1969 for the United States Senate Committee on Nutrition and Human Needs, discovered that the elimination of malnutrition (a major cause of disabling conditions) would benefit the country by an estimated $14 to $50 billion. Statistics like these prove the old adage, "An ounce of prevention is worth a pound of cure."

Aside from the economic consideration, there is a more important human consideration for the promotion of preventive health measures. There is a growing acceptance among health-care professionals and advocates in this country of the idea that every American should have the right to be "well-born" and the right to a good start in life. In order to achieve this goal, expanded programs of maternal and child health care and public education regarding preventive health care are needed.

Not all disabilities are congenital or strictly biological in origin. Many are the result of accident and, as new evidence continues to reveal, an increasing number of them are caused by environmental factors. Dr. John H. Knowles, president of the Rockefeller Foundation and editor of the book *Doing Better and Feeling Worse,* says, "Over 99 percent of us are born healthy and made sick as a result of personal misbehavior and environmental conditions."

Environmental pollution is a term we hear with increasing frequency as concern over the known and unknown effects of a host of potentially toxic substances in our environment grows. According to Russell E. Train, former administrator of the United States Environmental Protection Agency:

> The battle against disease must increasingly be fought, not simply in the hospitals and doctors' offices, but in our streets, homes and workplaces; in our air and water; in our food and products; and in our habits and lifestyles. Such a shift in emphasis will require a searching re-examination and radical revision of our popular understanding of, and our public approach to, health care and disease. If environmental disease is becoming "the disease of the century," as it appears to be, then environmental protection must become the most important ingredient in any national health program.

Air pollution, water pollution, noise pollution, chemical pollution are all by-products of our industrialized society. That is not to say that industry is bad or that modern technology is the cause of all illness and disability. Quite the contrary is true, for it is our advanced technology that has helped us produce ways of halting environmental pollution

The toxic by-products of industry, such as those emitted by this coke plant on the Monongahela River at Pittsburgh, are often the source of environmentally caused disability. (U.S. Environmental Protection Agency)

at its source. It is instead our unwillingness to apply our technology to this good end, and our rapid expansion of industry without thought being given to environmental consequences, that has proved detrimental to our national health.

Because it is often years, sometimes even generations, before the ill effects of a particular pollutant show in human beings, it is difficult for many of us to comprehend the full impact environmental pollution has on our health. Many substances that produce no ill effects in adults who come in contact with them can cause damage to the fetus within the pregnant woman. These substances, such as mercury and thalidomide, are known as *teratogens*. One of the disturbing things about teratogens is that their potential for harm has rarely proven detectable in advance. Their harmful effects are known only after the damage has been done.

There are other chemical pollutants called *mutagens* that affect the genetic composition of human cells, and can cause defects in future generations. Radiation is an example of a mutagen. It is difficult to measure just how much exposure to mutagens in the environment human beings are able to tolerate.

Since in many instances it is the toxic by-products of industry that are the source of environmentally caused disability, the factory or workplace has become a kind of pollution laboratory. The workers have become the unknowing victims of the harmful effects of certain poisonous substances. In an extensive survey of occupational hazards conducted by the National Institute of Occupational Safety and Health between 1972 and 1974, it was found that one American worker in four is exposed to some substance while on the job that may cause death or disease.

Human beings have faced hazards at work since the beginning of history. They have accepted these hazards, not necessarily willingly, but because they came with the job. Coal miners have always had lung trouble; steelworkers have always suffered from the heat of the furnace; and "accidents" have always occurred in the factory or the plant. In recent years, workers have been afflicted with a more exotic array of physical symptoms ranging from nerve damage, behavioral disorders, tremors, and seizures to mental retardation and temporary sterility. These have resulted from contact with substances such as mercury, lead and asbestos, and pesticides such as kepone and velsicol. Since it may take as long as thirty years from the time of initial exposure before a particular disorder shows up, it may be decades before we know just how much harm a particular pollutant can cause.

Be that as it may, there is much that we do know about the cause-and-effect relationship between the industrial environment and disability. We have the expertise to prevent many disabilities from occurring, but direct action against a particular problem has not always followed identification of it. For example, it is estimated that the federal government spends $1 billion a year treating the victims of black-lung disease, which afflicts coal miners, although the means to wipe out the disease existed thirty years ago.

Another example involves hearing loss. It is known that continued exposure to high noise levels can cause hearing loss. Yet it is estimated that nearly 40 million persons work in an environment noisy enough to damage their hearing

Continued exposure to high noise levels can cause hearing loss and contribute to other disabling conditions. (U.S. Environmental Protection Agency)

after prolonged exposure. In addition, a noisy workplace can contribute to other disabling conditions. A Ford Foundation report, *Crisis in the Workplace,* states:

> Noise is probably the most pervasive occupational hazard. . . . Noise is a stressor and may therefore be responsible for increased incidence of heart disease. Noise may very well be a cocausative factor in diseases associated with toxic material in general.
>
> Noise also reduces the level of visual acuity with the result that the cost of accidents is likely to be higher in noisy shops.

These are but two of the more striking examples of the many preventable hazards that continue to exist in the workplace. A Labor Department report has estimated that in the last half of 1971, out of a total work force of 57 million, there were 3.1 million recordable job-related injuries and illnesses. A 1972 *President's Report on Occupational Safety and Health* stated that "there may be as many as 100,000 deaths per year from occupationally caused diseases . . . and at least 390,000 new cases of disabling occupational diseases each year." These are probably conservative estimates since many such accidents and illnesses are not immediately recognized or recorded as work-related.

Why do preventable accidents, injuries, and disease continue to wreak havoc in the workplace? Primarily, say labor and government officials, because industry chooses to cut back on safety measures for economy's sake.

25

In 1969 the Williams-Steiger Occupational Safety and Health Act was voted into law by Congress "to assure so far as possible every working man and woman in the nation safe and healthful working conditions and to preserve our human resources." This act legislated standards of safety that employers had been unwilling to adopt on their own. The act requires that

> Each employer shall furnish to each of his employees employment and a place of employment which are free from recognized hazards that are causing or are likely to cause death or serious harm to his employees, and shall comply with occupational safety and health standards issued under the act.

The Williams-Steiger Act provided for the establishment of the Occupational Safety and Health Administration (OSHA) within the Department of Labor. This agency is responsible for setting safety and health standards in the workplace and insuring that employers comply with them. A National Institute for Occupational Safety and Health was also set up within the Department of Health, Education, and Welfare. Its responsibilities include the study of the problem of occupational hazards and the discovery of new methods of dealing with them.

So far the Williams-Steiger Act has had little impact. Funding for the implementation of the bill has come to only approximately one dollar per worker (about $57 million). As a result OSHA and related agencies cannot afford the manpower needed to properly inform employers of standards and to see to it that they comply with them.

A growing number of disabled workers have begun to take matters into their own hands, and have brought suit against their employers and the government agencies involved in overseeing occupational safety and health. Four hundred asbestos workers who contracted asbestosis (a lung disease caused by the inhalation of asbestos fibers) have brought suit against the Department of Health, Education, and Welfare. They argue that they contracted this often fatal disease because, although the government knew of the hazards involved, it failed to give them timely warning about the danger of exposure on their jobs.

In another court action, eight California workers brought suit against a former company physician, alleging that the company knowingly exposed workers to excessive concentrations of a substance known to cause cancer.

This kind of suit is likely to become more commonplace unless Congress acts to enforce present safety standards and /or comes up with more effective legislation and standards that will compel industry to take responsibility for the health of its workers, and the protection of the environment.

A statement made by Leonard Woodcock, former president of the United Auto Workers Union, regarding noise pollution in the workplace, can be applied to all preventable occupational hazards. He said:

Industry's complaints of high cost are self-serving and highly inflated. New technology and mass production of noise-control devices will cut present costs dramatically. Industry has survived a host of other needed social reforms, and [it] will survive the elimination of noises.

Of course the best way to deal with the problem is to prevent disability from occurring, and when it has occurred, to prevent it from worsening. Although we know a great deal about the causes of many physiological disorders, there is still much that we do not know. If a right to prevention and alleviation of disability for all Americans is our goal, then a continued search for new knowledge must be supported. Research must go hand in glove with prevention, for without one we cannot achieve the other. Intensive research is needed in the areas of reproductive biology and fetal development, disease, and the effects of drugs and toxic chemicals that are now routinely released into the environment.

In addition, new methods of relieving the handicapping effects of disability must be sought out. There have been some spectacular developments in the field of biomedical engineering in recent years. These include breath- and eye-controlled wheelchairs, artificial limbs that function almost like real ones, artificial bone joints, artificial vision, print-to-speech devices and telephone aids for the immobile and the hard of hearing. Most of these devices are still in the experimental stage, and many more years of research and development are needed before they can be made available to the general market.

Our attitudes toward disability and methods of dealing with its causes are gradually changing, as are our feelings with regard to health care in general in this country. We are coming to realize, as Dr. Theodore Cooper, former assistant secretary for health in the Department of Health, Education, and Welfare, wrote, that "medicine is an art and a science concerned as much with preserving health as restoring it." Awareness of the need for and the possibility of preventing hazardous disabling conditions is reflected in the current widespread interest in environmental protection, consumer protection, and job safety. It is hoped that this new trend will result in the increased application of known measures of prevention and a renewed commitment to the search for those as yet unknown, so that in the future millions of Americans will be spared the handicap of preventable physical disability.

The Right to Treatment

The handicapped individual has the right to health services and medical care for the protection of his general well-being and such additional special services as are required because of his handicap.

—A BILL OF RIGHTS FOR THE HANDICAPPED,
United Cerebral Palsy Associations

When Dr. Wilkins slid back the heavy metal door of B Ward, Building No. 6, the horrible smell of the place staggered me. It was so wretched that my first thought was that the air was poisonous and would kill me. I looked down to steady myself and I saw a freak: a grotesque caricature of a person, lying under a sink on an incredibly filthy tile floor in an incredibly filthy bathroom. It was wearing trousers, but they were pulled down around the ankles. It was skinny. It was twisted. It was lying in its own feces, and it wasn't alone. Sitting next to this thing was another freak. In a parody of human emotions, they were holding hands. They were making a noise. It was a wailing sound that I still hear and that I will never forget. I said out loud, but to nobody in particular, "My God, they're children."

The preceding paragraph is not a description of a nineteenth-century asylum, or "snakepit," but the account of a news reporter's reactions to the appalling conditions he discovered on his first visit to an institution for the mentally retarded in 1972. The reporter was Geraldo Rivera, and the scene he so vividly depicts occurred at the Willowbrook School for the Mentally Retarded on Staten Island. At the time of his visit, Willowbrook was the nation's largest facility for the mentally retarded, housing over five thousand people.

While gathering information for a television news program on conditions at Willowbrook, which was to shock the nation, Mr. Rivera found stark filthy wards, some with sixty to seventy children crowded into them. More often than not, there was only one attendant to care for all the children in a ward. Most of the children were either naked or clothed in tatters. Some were in straitjackets, while others lay passively on the floor, drugged into a zombie-like stupor so that they could be more easily managed by the overworked staff. Many of the children had cuts, bruises, and burns on their bodies. Repulsed by what he saw, Mr. Rivera went on to write: "The kids were disgusting to look at and their sound made me want to put my hands over my ears, but the smell was what made me physically sick. It smelled of filth. It smelled of disease. And it smelled of death."

Senator Robert F. Kennedy had this to say after a visit to an institution for the mentally retarded: "[In] state institutions for the retarded . . . I think . . . that we have a situation that borders on a snakepit. . . . [There is] very little future for . . . children who are in these institutions."

Unfortunately, Willowbrook is not an isolated case. It is typical of conditions at far too many public institutions for the mentally retarded. The purpose of these institutions is, supposedly, the care and treatment of the mentally retarded, but very little care and treatment can be provided in facilities that are overcrowded, understaffed, and underfunded. Such institutions are little better than warehouses for wasted human lives, where the care is custodial at best, and often outright abusive.

Because they are underfunded, many institutions for the mentally retarded are overcrowded and understaffed. (The President's Committee on Mental Retardation)

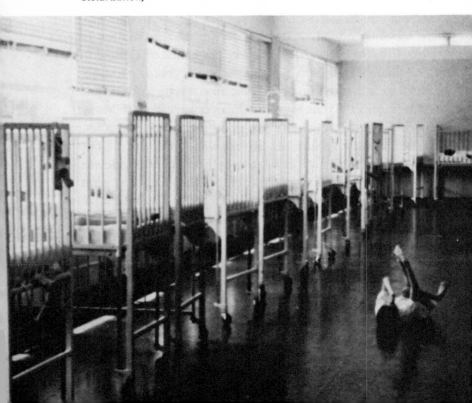

In 1970 a fourteen-year-old boy drowned in a shower in a residential facility in Pennsylvania. In another institution in the same state, children were put in wooden cages as a means of punishment. In some instances institution residents have been used as "guinea pigs" in medical research. Over-prescription of drugs, unsanitary conditions, poor diet, inadequate medical attention, and lack of privacy are commonplace in many public institutions. In recent years a number of court cases have been brought on behalf of residents in state institutions who have suffered personal injuries and sexual assault.

Such cruel and inhuman treatment in public institutions has prompted a number of lawsuits since 1960. The most important to the establishment of a legal right to treatment for the disabled is the case of *Wyatt v. Stickney*. This class-action suit was brought in 1970 on behalf of all mentally ill and mentally retarded persons involuntarily confined in institutions in the state of Alabama. For the first time the courts upheld the constitutional right of persons so confined to adequate treatment and habilitation. After hearing expert witnesses testify that conditions in Alabama state institutions resulted in the "deterioration" and the "debilitation" rather than the rehabilitation of those confined to them, Judge Frank Johnson stated: "To deprive any citizen of his or her liberty upon the altruistic theory that the confinement is for humane therapeutic reasons and then to fail to provide adequate treatment violates the very fundamentals of due process."

The judge was saying that if the need for treatment is given as the purpose for confinement in an institution, then the patient has a constitutional right under the due-process provision of the Fourteenth Amendment to receive treatment. Judge Johnson went on to stress that such treatment must occur in an environment that meets certain humane physical and psychological standards and that "the mentally retarded have a constitutional right to receive such individual habilitation as will give each of them a realistic opportunity to lead a more useful and meaningful life and to return to society." In other words, simple maintenance of the individual is not enough. Some effort must be made to improve his condition.

In addition to due process, there are several other constitutional principles that have been used to argue the right to treatment. The "equal protection" clause of the Fourteenth Amendment has been cited along with the Eighth Amendment's prohibition against "cruel and unusual punishment." The Supreme Court has ruled that confinement of a mentally disabled individual without treatment is a kind of punishment, and is therefore in violation of this Eighth Amendment prohibition.

Violations of the Thirteenth Amendment's guarantee of freedom from "involuntary servitude" have been cited in cases brought by residents of institutions who were forced to work without pay in the maintenance of their institutions. (This kind of action will be discussed in greater detail in Chapter 6.)

Another legal precedent cited in the *Wyatt* case and in other right-to-treatment suits is the principle of "least drastic means," which was first put forth by the United States Supreme Court in its ruling in the case of *Shelton v. Tucker* in 1960. It states:

Even though the governmental purpose be legitimate and substantial, that purpose cannot be pursued by means that broadly stifle fundamental personal liberties when the end can be more narrowly achieved. The breadth of legislative abridgement must be viewed in the light of less drastic means for achieving the same basic purpose.

In other words, if the state is going to restrict a person's freedom by placing him in an institution, for example, the state has the responsibility to keep such restriction to a minimum. Applying this principle in the *Wyatt* case, Judge Johnson ruled that mentally retarded persons in need of treatment should receive it in a setting that is the least restrictive to their personal liberty and as close to normal as possible. In the landmark civil-commitment case of *Lessard v. Schmidt* (1972), it was decided that involuntary institutionalization should be considered only as a [treatment of] last resort.

The courts in the *Wyatt* case and related suits have established a constitutional basis for the right to individualized treatment in the most humane and least restrictive setting possible. In addition, the courts have found that a state's objection that it lacks the facilities or the means to comply with these rulings does not justify the withholding of appropriate treatment. In the Texas right-to-treatment case, *Morales v. Turman* (1976), the court decreed:

The state may not circumvent the Constitution by simply refusing to create any alternatives to incarceration;

A staff member from The Lighthouse of the New York Association for the Blind follows several steps behind a young blind woman who is learning to maneuver busy city streets and sidewalks for herself. (The Lighthouse of the New York Association for the Blind)

it must act affirmatively to foster such alternatives as now exist only in rudimentary form, and to build new programs suited to the needs of the hundreds of its children that do not need institutional care. . . .

When the state of Alabama balked at making changes in line with the federal court's ruling in the *Wyatt* case, the federal court intervened and took over the operation of Alabama's state hospitals. Similar action has been taken by courts in Louisiana and Mississippi.

This kind of "judicial activism" has caused a good deal of controversy among legal and public officials. Many of them, particularly the governor and members of the Alabama state legislature, viewed Judge Johnson's action as a gross overextension of his judicial power, and an encroachment on the powers of the legislative and executive branches of government. But Judge Johnson has countered their criticism with the following declaration:

In an ideal society, all of these judgments and decisions should be made by those to whom we have entrusted these responsibilities. But when governmental institutions fail to make these judgements and decisions in a manner which comports with the Constitution, the Federal courts have a duty to remedy the violation.

The controversy continues to rage in Georgia, Minnesota, Massachusetts, Nebraska, Illinois, and New York, where similar class-action suits have been filed. In 1972, parents filed a class-action suit against the Willowbrook State School mentioned at the beginning of this chapter. As a result of a consent agreement reached in 1975, the terrible conditions caused by overcrowding at Willowbrook are being relieved by the gradual transferral of the majority of the children to smaller community-based residences. In the case of *Burnham v. the State of Georgia,* the court "respectfully disagreed" with the findings in the *Wyatt* case. The judge in the *Burnham* case ruled that while there might possibly be a moral obligation to provide treatment to patients confined in state institutions, there was no clearly judicially enforceable constitutional right to treatment. And five years after Judge Johnson's ruling in the *Wyatt* case, Alabama's state institutions still failed to comply fully with the terms of his decree.

It is a long slow process, but gradually the courts, the government, and the people are coming to accept the idea of a disabled person's right to receive treatment, and have even extended that right to include rehabilitation. In the narrow sense of the word, treatment applies merely to the cure or lessening of the effects of a physical disorder. In most cases of permanent physical disability, however, the individual's needs go beyond the requirements of mere physical maintenance. Interpreted broadly, the concept of treatment for the disabled encompasses training and therapy that will assist the individual in developing to his full potential, no matter how narrow or limited that may be. For example, treatment for the retarded person could include such things as help in acquiring life skills, occupational therapy, and vocational training.

Unfortunately the system for providing treatment and rehabilitation for the disabled in this country continues to remain woefully inadequate to the need and far behind what

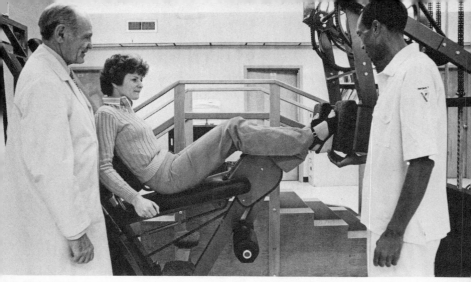

Physical therapy seeks to restore maximum functioning levels in physically disabled individuals. (ICD Rehabilitation and Research Center)

These adolescents are both mentally retarded and deaf. At the ICD Rehabilitation and Research Center in New York City, therapists work with them to assess their employment potential. (ICD Rehabilitation and Research Center)

have generally come to be considered acceptable standards since the *Wyatt* case. The major flaws in the present system of public services for the treatment of the disabled are:

—Rigid standardization of services, requiring the individual to adjust to the system rather than vice versa.
—Location of services in institutions isolated from the community.
—Lack of coordination in the administration of various services making it extremely difficult for the disabled individual to find the right program for himself.
—An information gap that leaves most of the disabled uninformed as to what kinds of services are available and how to obtain them.

These obstacles will have to be overcome if the disabled are to achieve their right to humane, accessible, and individualized treatment and rehabilitation, and ultimately the realization of their full human potential.

5

The Right to Education

The handicapped individual has the right to education to the fullest extent to which he is intellectually capable, provided through the regular channels of American education.

—A BILL OF RIGHTS FOR THE HANDICAPPED,
United Cerebral Palsy Associations

Michelle Duffy is a thirteen-year-old girl paralyzed from the waist down by a congenital disorder known as spina bifida, which means "open spine." She is confined to a wheelchair.

"When Michelle started school," her father said, "we assumed, like most parents of handicapped children, that our child would go to a special school. But for the two years she was there, we were never pleased and thought that the special setting was holding her back."

In spite of the warnings of "specialists," Michelle's parents took her out of the special school and placed her in a regular class in the public-school system. Mr. Duffy said, "I'm down on special schools for children like Michelle. These kids get so much individual attention and the classes are so small that the kids are really unprepared for the larger world. The public schools do that kind of preparation for other children. There is no reason they should not do it for handicapped children—even kids who are very handicapped like Michelle."

Michelle Duffy is lucky. According to a report published by the United States Office of Education in 1975, about half of our country's 7,800,000 handicapped children between the ages of three and twenty-one are not receiving an adequate education. Approximately 1,000,000 of them are not receiving any education at all.

As discouraging as these statistics may appear, they do represent a substantial improvement over previous years. Still more important is the dramatic change that has taken place in our attitude with regard to the place of the disabled within our educational system. In fact, access to public education is the area in which disabled activists have been making the most progress.

In the earliest years of our nation, the disabled were generally considered uneducable and were for the most part kept at home where they received no education at all. It was not until the beginning of the nineteenth century that some effort was made to educate disabled children. The first such attempts took place in charitable asylums. Later, special residential schools were created to serve children according to their particular disability. There were special schools for the deaf, the blind, and the "feeble-minded," as the retarded were called in those days. These first private schools received their support from charitable and religious organizations. Later, the various state departments of health or social

42

welfare began to set up residential schools of their own.

It was not until the close of the nineteenth century that disabled children began gradually to make their way into the public-school system. This change came about as a result of overcrowding in residential schools and the introduction of compulsory education laws in the states. Special classes for the mildly handicapped were created within public schools as an alternative to residential schools. Disabled children, however, continued to be excluded from regular classrooms, where they were considered "out of place" and an actual deterrent to the education of the other students.

In the beginning of this century, some farsighted educators began to include handicapped children in the regular classrooms. This action gave rise to a period of questioning among educators regarding the effectiveness of so-called special education that kept the disabled segregated from other children. About the time that the concept of "mainstreaming," that is, the integration of disabled students into regular classrooms, began to gain wide acceptance, the United States Supreme Court handed down its unanimous decision in the *Brown v. Board of Education* case. This 1954 landmark ruling involving the segregation of black students established the right to education for all children, and declared that "separate but equal" educational facilities were detrimental to the learning process, and, therefore, totally unacceptable. Taking their lead from the *Brown* case, groups of parents of disabled children went to the courts to sue for the protection of their children's right to an education. In 1971 the Pennsylvania Association for Retarded Children brought a class-action suit in federal court against the Commonwealth of Pennsylvania *(PARC v. Commonwealth of Pennsylvania)* on behalf of fourteen retarded children who had been denied a free public education. This suit directly challenged Pennsylvania laws that denied access to public education to those judged "ineducable." When confronted with expert testimony that proved overwhelmingly that all children are to some degree educable, the state of Pennsylvania entered into a "consent agreement" with the plaintiffs. (When the opposing parties in a lawsuit agree upon what needs to be done about the issue in question, they are said to have reached a "consent agreement.")

In its decree, the federal court acknowledged for the first time the right of mentally retarded children to equal access to public education. In addition, in accordance with constitutional due-process requirements, the court specifically ordered that no child's educational status could be changed without his parents being given proper advance notice and the opportunity to oppose that change in a formal hearing. This meant, for example, that a school could not assign a child to a special-education class without notifying his parents first and allowing them to challenge that decision in court if necessary. The court also set forth specific priorities for the educational placement of retarded children. It declared: "Placement in a regular public school classroom is preferable to placement in a special public school class. . . ." Home instruction was the third alternative, and placement in a residential institution was to be considered only as a last resort. As with the right to treatment, the court upheld the concept of a right to education in the "least restrictive" environment.

The *PARC* case is a landmark in the establishment of a right to education for the retarded. Certain points made in the court-approved consent agreement set precedents for later educational innovations. The agreement reads in part:

> . . . mentally retarded persons are capable of benefitting from a program of education and training; the greatest number of retarded persons, given such education and training are capable of achieving self-sufficiency, and the remaining few, with such education and training are capable of achieving some degree of self-care; that the earlier such education and training begins, the more thoroughly and the more efficiently the mentally retarded person will benefit from it; and, whether begun early or not, that a mentally retarded person can benefit at any point in his life and development from the program of education and training.

The decision in the 1972 class-action suit, *Mills v. Board of Education of District of Columbia,* picked up where the *PARC* ruling left off. It applied not only to the mentally retarded, but to all individuals with any kind of emotional or physical disability. Basing its decision on the due-process and equal-protection clauses of the Constitution, the court established the constitutional right to a free, publicly supported education for all handicapped children. In addition, the court held that a plea of insufficient funds was no excuse for withholding education from the disabled. In his decision, Judge Joseph Waddy made it clear that:

> If sufficient funds are not available to finance all of the services and programs that are needed in the system, then the available funds must be expended equitably in such a manner that no child is entirely excluded from a publicly supported education consistent with his needs and ability to benefit therefrom.

Since the *PARC* and *Mills* decisions, dozens of similar suits have been brought in at least twenty-five states, and most, if not all, of the cases that have reached completion have been decided in favor of the disabled children involved. In the 1976 case, *Hairston v. Drosick,* involving a disabled child denied admission to a regular classroom, the judge, in his ruling, placed great emphasis on the crucial importance of educational mainstreaming to the lifelong development of the disabled. He said:

> A child's chance in this society is through the educational process. A major goal of the educational process is the socialization process that takes place in the regular classroom, with the resulting capacity to interact in a social way with one's peers. It is, therefore, imperative that every child receive an education with his or her peers insofar as it is at all possible. This conclusion is further enforced by the critical importance of education in this society. . . . It is an educational fact that the

maximum benefits to a child are received by placement in as normal an environment as possible.

This kind of litigation has led to legislative action on both the state and federal levels. Today, all fifty states have laws that provide some kind of educational services for disabled children; and since 1965 the United States Congress has added steadily to its list of right-to-education legislation.

In 1965 the Elementary and Secondary Education Act was passed. Title I of that act specifically included the handicapped. Five years and several bills on special education later, the Education of the Handicapped Act (PL 91-230) was passed. The Education Amendments of 1974 (PL 93-380), however, was the real watershed in this type of legislation. Taking its lead from the courts, Congress cited the due-process requirement in the educational placement of disabled children, called for the least restrictive and closest to normal setting for the education of the handicapped, and required that each state formulate a plan for the inclusion of all its handicapped in its educational services. Receipt of federal funding for education of the handicapped was made dependent on approval of the new state plan.

The 1975 Education for All Handicapped Children Act (PL 94-142) strengthened and broadened the coverage of the Education Amendments of 1974. It specifically required that each state insure a "free appropriate public education" and an "individualized education program" to all its handicapped children ages three to eighteen by September 1, 1978, and to all its handicapped children ages three to twenty-one by September 1, 1980. In addition, the Education for All Handicapped Children Act expanded the federal government's ideological and financial commitment to the right of the disabled to education.

In sum, the right to education for the disabled established by litigation and legislation calls for a commitment to:

—Access for all handicapped children to free public education
—Educational programming designed to fit the needs of the individual
—Education that occurs in the least restrictive and most constructive setting
—Due-process protection in educational placement
—Periodic review of the individual's program of education and placement within the system
—Expansion of our present concept of education to comply with the total life requirements of the disabled.

"Mainstreaming" is perhaps the most controversial and certainly the most attention-getting of all the elements in the establishment of a right to education for the disabled.

Public schools have traditionally been designed to meet the needs of the average normal child. Those who do not fit into that category have been relegated to the special school, or special class, that was separated from the regular school or class. The law now specifically requires that a majority of children formerly relegated to "special" education, or no education at all, must now be accommodated in the regular classroom.

Putting this legislative mandate into action will require nothing short of a revolution in our present educational system. It has already created a situation that is causing a great deal of concern among teachers. Many teachers feel that in their rush to integrate handicapped students into the regular classroom in compliance with the law, the states have not taken into consideration the fact that, as Sol Levine, vice-president of New York City's United Federation of Teachers, put it, "The average teacher is trained to teach only the average child."

Fred Andelman of the Massachusetts Teachers' Association adds:

It's fine to pass laws, but it's the teachers who are stuck trying to implement them. . . . a lot of teachers have no experience in dealing with handicapped kids. . . . If there are going to be laws like this, they should be taken into account during a teacher's education.

In order for mainstreaming to be effective, handicapped children cannot simply be "dumped" into regular classrooms. Teachers must be trained to deal with the special needs of their disabled students; the handicapped student must be prepared for his transfer from special education to regular education; and each school must be equipped to provide individualized instruction for its disabled students.

With careful planning and cooperation between parents

and teachers, mainstreaming can be a boon to everyone involved. One mother of a seven-and-a-half-year-old described her experience this way:

> He started kindergarten . . . as one of twenty-six in a crowded classroom . . . in our home town. . . .
>
> We sent him, not knowing how he would react, but hoping that he would adapt well enough to continue to go and learn. The fact that he did adjust happily, enjoyed attending the class and cooperated in group activities is, we feel, due to the sympathetic understanding, kindness, and patience of his teacher. . . .

The mother of a blind girl describes some of the advantages of a mainstreamed class for her daughter:

> Sometimes, watching her with the others, I remembered the blind children playing in the residential nursery, each child all by himself. Blind children play together more slowly. Time is lost just in hunting for things and for each other. It is quite a feat even for one blind child to give another a cookie. First he has to find the child, then his hand, and put the cookie into it.
>
> Eileen with her sighted friends just holds out her hand with the cookie in it, says "Here you are!" and the thing is done. Also, Eileen's sighted friends are constantly attracted to things about them. A tumblebug, a red flower, or passing fire engine are all thrilling, and sighted children volubly draw each other's attention

from one attraction to the next. Eileen is introduced to many fascinating items she would otherwise not notice or understand.

Eileen's mother expressed the desire that her daughter continue "to go to a public school with normal children and . . . have only a few classes with the blind. When she is through school, we hope she will be able to face the world along with her sighted contemporaries and make her own way."

Individualized instruction is a concept that has been advocated by many educators of the nonhandicapped as well as the handicapped for years. All students would benefit from a system that educated them according to their individual abilities and needs, and at their own rates of learning. A system that is flexible and that can accommodate all children is vastly preferable to one which requires that a variety of children with a variety of special needs accommodate themselves to its rigid standards.

Traditionally children have been routinely rated and evaluated near the beginning of their educational careers. This early testing and assessment often determined the entire course of a child's education, which, in turn, affected his future progress in society.

This kind of permanent labeling often stigmatized handicapped children without serving any real educational purpose. The abuse of the I.Q. test is the most obvious example of the harmful effects of this kind of practice. Once that test had been administered, and its score marked on a child's permanent record, his progress along the educational, social, and employment ladder was pretty well predetermined. This was especially true of the disabled.

Under the new legislation, this kind of early educational predetermination is to be abolished. Each child's progress and ability will be measured at periodic intervals throughout his schooling. Children will no longer be doomed to a single track in life because they had been labeled "retarded" or "ineducable" on the basis of one or two tests taken at a very early age.

The expansion of our traditional approach to education to include students and subjects previously considered outside the range of our system of public education is one of the most significant changes called for in recent right-to-education legislation and litigation. When considering education for the disabled, it is necessary to think beyond mere schooling for a limited age-group in a fixed environment. As one of the experts testifying in the *PARC* case put it: "Education is a continuous process of developing life skills needed for the effective coping with developmental tasks and demands as well as with environmental tasks and demands."

In other words, education should be an open-ended continuum available from the cradle to the grave that serves individual needs. In the case of the disabled, individual need often extends beyond the realm of the "three R's." In a 1976 New York court case involving a mentally retarded girl's education, the court recognized that education involves different things for different children. According to the court ruling, a mentally retarded child requires another kind of "education"—how to hold a spoon, feed herself, dress herself, toilet training, et cetera, in addition to speech therapy, psychiatric and psychological treatment, et cetera—all these and more add up to the education of this and other mentally retarded children, and they are entitled to be so educated.

Early childhood developmental assistance and preschool education at one end of the age spectrum, and continuing education and training programs at the other, should be available to all who can benefit from them. Growth does not start at age three and end at age twenty-one. It is a continuous life process and educational programs that assist that growth should be there for those who need them.

In the home management center at the Human Resources Center, Albertson, Long Island, New York, these disabled children learn skills that enable them to live more independently in their own home environments. (Human Resources Center)

Although continuing education and adult education have been part of our educational system for years, there have been very few such programs in regular schools geared to the special needs and interests of the mentally retarded or physically disabled. Only two colleges in the United States—the State University of New York at Brockport and Broward Community College in Fort Lauderdale, Florida—offer continuing education for mentally retarded adults as part of their regular curriculum.

SUNY at Brockport offers a program called "Basic Skills for Independent Living," which features courses that help the mentally retarded develop the social skills they need to function independently in our society. Broward's "Educational Program for Exceptional Adults" focuses on the development of job skills, social skills, and personal interests. According to Dr. Eileen Corcoran, director of the Brockport program, "Each retarded person has a right to function as fully as he can in his community. The continuing-education program at the local college is the logical place for the retarded student to begin."

In addition to expanding education to include training for the disabled in life skills, many educators agree that special attention should be given to providing the disabled with access to experiences that are life-enhancing. The classroom is not the only setting where the learning process takes place, and the school alone cannot bear the burden of enriching the lives of the disabled. A disabled child, like any other child, needs more than practical skills and intellectual knowledge if he is to live a full, rich, rewarding life. Teachers and their disabled students must also look to recreational facilities and

This crippled child is a participant in a summer camp program. (Human Resources Center)

sports arenas, to art studios and museums, the theater and concert halls.

In recent years, a number of museums and art galleries have begun presenting special shows and exhibits that are of particular interest to handicapped visitors. So-called Touch Me exhibits, designed especially for the blind and physically handicapped and featuring objects and works of art that are meant to be explored tactilely, have been very popular among the nondisabled as well as the disabled. There are at present only about twenty locations in the country where such programs are regularly presented.

In July 1977, the Metropolitan Museum of Art in New York presented an exhibit titled "Shape and Form: A Tactile Exploration" that included forty art objects—sculptures, tiles, textiles—that visitors were invited to feel. Lawrence Brown, director of the Children's Museum of Denver, had the following to say about the value of such exhibitions:

> Most museums are browsing museums where people walk the halls and look. It's an aesthetic experience. Everything is behind glass and two-dimensional. In order to have a real three-dimensional experience, it's necessary to have objects out there you can sense.

The fine arts can play an important part in the handicapped child's classroom experience as well. Innovative educators have come to recognize the potential of the arts in the improvement of perceptual and mechanical skills, the encouragement of positive responses to outside stimuli, and the development of untapped creative abilities in handicapped children.

The National Endowment for the Arts has sponsored a number of programs through grants that have proven the value of arts instruction to the handicapped. One such program called "Artists in Schools" (AIS) provides states with funds for placing working artists in classrooms. A 1975–76 study of ten states that took advantage of the AIS program demonstrated the positive effect of the program on handicapped students.

The study reports that children with learning problems often showed even more creativity and interest than other children when artists worked with them . . . passive and emotionally disturbed children increased their verbal and self-expressive activities. . . . Poets observed that poetry writing was therapeutic for the students and produced an improvement in their self-confidence and self-discipline. Moreover, the classroom teachers observed improvement in student interest and achievement in other academic areas.

The mother of a mentally retarded boy writes of his experience with music:

Often retarded children have a special love of music. As soon as it developed that music and rhythm were departments in which Stephen really had a talent, [his teacher] gave him frequent opportunities to display this ability. We feel that the lift to his ego and the prestige that he gained in the eyes of the other children were beyond the possibility of evaluation.

. . . it is thrilling to watch a situation where [retarded children] are allowed to come into the sunlight. They need every encouragement, every chance to do things well. How can they be brought to the fulfillment of their . . . abilities unless opportunities are given them?

In 1976 a Connecticut organizaton known as Project SEARCH (Search for Exceptional Abilities Reachable Among Children with Handicaps) found that 12 percent of the handicapped children they tested were gifted artistically. What makes this discovery so extraordinary is the fact that this percentage is roughly three times that expected in the general school population.

Under the program, professional artists travel to schools throughout the state to supplement instruction in the visual arts, music, and movement to handicapped children, ages six to fifteen. According to SEARCH project director, Allen J. White, the program gives artistically gifted handicapped children

> a chance to do something they're good at instead of focusing on areas where there are problems. Even children who don't have exceptional ability could benefit from this kind of program [because] there is no right or wrong answer to problems in the creative arts. Many of the activities that we do to foster creative expression and creative development are so open-ended that children with lesser abilities than those we've identified can also respond and participate in them in a satisfying way.

Physical health and well-being are also important to all-around personal development, and an integral part of any education program. For many of the disabled, physical fitness is absolutely essential. The benefits of physical-fitness and sports programs designed for the disabled go beyond the merely physical. The psychological reward of knowing one

Basketball was the first organized wheelchair competition sport. This scene is from the 22nd annual National Wheelchair Basketball Tournament between the Detroit Sparks and the University of Illinois Gizz Kids. (University of Illinois Rehabilitation–Education Center, Champaign, Illinois, through courtesy of the American Alliance for Health, Physical Education, and Recreation)

can control one's body and a sense of personal achievement are tremendously important to the development of the disabled individual. What happens in the gym, the pool, or on the playing field can have a direct, positive effect on what goes on in the classroom.

Most disabled students, however, are routinely excluded from physical-education programs in schools, and some are taking legal action to change regulations that prevent their full participation. In 1976, two junior high school students, Margaret Kampmeier and Steven Gineco, brought suit against public school officials in upstate New York because they were denied permission to participate in contact sports.

Margaret has a congenital cataract in one eye, and Steven is nearly blind in one eye from an injury that occurred when he was six. Both had been very active in sports throughout their schooling, in spite of their disabilities. Steven had played football and basketball, and Margaret, who wore special safety glasses to protect her eyes while participating in sports, was one of the best athletes in her class.

During the 1975–76 school year they were prohibited from participating in contact sports by the school physician because, according to school regulations, blindness in one eye automatically disqualified them from sports, even though their past record had proven them fully capable of participation. The court in this case agreed with school officials who argued that it was their responsibility to protect the well-being of their students in general, and Margaret and Steven in particular, from the high risk of further eye injury in contact sports.

In trying to establish a right to education for the handicapped, our nation's lawmakers and educators have outlined several educational innovations that would benefit everyone, whether disabled or nondisabled, who passed through our public-education system. Each student would come in contact with new and different people and places, and he would enjoy experiences he never would have within the traditional system.

But many educators and public officials complain that the costs of such innovations will be extremely high, and that it will be difficult, if not impossible, for most already financially overburdened school districts to absorb them. Altering school buildings to make them accessible to handicapped students, training teachers to cope with the special needs of the handicapped, creating individualized education plans for each handicapped child, providing a full range of extracurricular activities for the handicapped, are all costly undertakings. Some estimates of the costs of these additional services run as high as $3 billion. This is over and above the annual $12 billion nationwide cost of education.

However, in testimony before the House Subcommittee on Select Education in September of 1977, Thomas P. Carroll, executive director of the National Center for Law and the Handicapped, called such cost estimates "unrealistically exaggerated," and said that "the financial objections . . . are specious . . . we cannot afford to permit these financial complaints . . . as premature and undocumented as they are, to interfere with the guarantees of the civil rights of [the] handicapped. . . ."

At the University of Alabama, a student finds aisles in the library wide enough for his wheelchair. (The President's Committee on Employment of the Handicapped)

Those who complain about the short-term expense of such dramatic innovations should look instead at the long-term human gains as well as the economic ones. Keeping handicapped children segregated in institutions and special-education classes is itself costly. According to Dr. Robert Audette, associate commissioner for special education in Massachusetts, "It costs $400,000 to maintain one person in an institution for life. This money would be much better spent trying to make everyone a productive member of society."

It has been estimated that if only a fraction of disabled children were removed from special institutions and special classrooms and mainstreamed into regular classrooms, the economic saving would amount to hundreds of millions of dollars a year. It is impossible to measure the savings in once-wasted human lives, but it stands to reason that an educated, productive, self-sufficient person is an asset to society. Everyone should have the right to the education and training needed to come as close to that goal as he is able.

Michelle Duffy is doing well in public school, despite predictions that she would not be accepted by the other children and that teachers would not be able to cope with her. ". . . none of these things has happened," says Michelle's father. "Instead, in the . . . schools Michelle has attended, teachers and administrators have made provisions for her and have enjoyed working with her." Mr. Duffy adds, ". . . it's a terrible mistake to pack these kids off in one place. A special school is a nice convenient way to get them out of sight. But this practice does nothing to solve the problems society has in dealing effectively with handicapped people."

63

The Right to Employment
and Compensation

The handicapped individual has the right to work at any occupation for which he has the qualifications and preparation; an income sufficient to maintain a lifestyle comparable to his non-handicapped peers.

—A BILL OF RIGHTS FOR THE HANDICAPPED,
United Cerebral Palsy Associations

EMPLOYMENT

Phillip A. suffers from a fused spine and neck which makes it impossible for him to sit, yet he works as a drill-press operator.

Peter A.'s left arm was severed above the elbow and his right hand cut off at the wrist when he was a boy. Today he works as a stock foreman.

"Shorty" D. lost his lower legs when a car he was repairing slipped off the jack and severed them. He now works as a cement finisher.

John L. performs his job as the vice-president and assistant to the chairman of one of the world's largest airlines from a wheelchair.

Jim A., an industrial designer, has an artificial hand.

James H. is bedridden due to paralysis of the legs and other physical problems, but he continues his work as an accountant.

These people all have two things in common: they are disabled, and they are employed. They are the exception to the rule.

Most disabled people seeking employment have problems similar to the young woman with epilepsy who wrote to her congressman:

Dear Sir:
It is my belief that productive work is a true good of life, a contributor to one's self-esteem, manufactured as we produce for others.

For many years now I have lived in hopes of being able to be a producer in my society. Earning my M.S. degree through part-time employment, I hoped for the day when I would be able to apply this education. I find in America, however, that the employers are still reluctant to accept the handicapped and let us build our self-esteem and produce for them.

When one makes application for a position, he no longer has to admit his desire or intention to work against his government, yet I must admit to a physical handicap which in no way would hinder the perform-ance I could and would render. Suddenly this admission causes me to be classified as "overqualified" or given some other reason for not being hired.

. . . I cannot do what I want to do most—WORK. What suggestions have you for me and the others like me who must be costing the country much wasted gray matter? Can't we be given an opportunity to contribute?

This woman's situation is typical of many handicapped Americans of working age who are either unemployed or underemployed. It has been estimated that two out of three handicapped adults never find permanent jobs. This is the case in spite of the fact that 78 percent have at least an eighth-grade education, and another 5 percent are college graduates. According to a study based on the 1970 United States Census, 52 percent have annual incomes below $2,000. This means that the proportion of handicapped individuals living below the poverty level is twice as high as that of the nondisabled population.

The physically disabled have been regularly denied access to paid employment throughout our nation's history, because it was felt that they were incompetent and unable to produce at a level competitive with that of the normal worker. Those few who managed to make it into the general labor market have done so chiefly in the lowest-paying unskilled jobs where they were always vulnerable to lay-offs.

For years the main source of employment for the disabled was found in the residential institutions in which they were segregated. There they were put to work doing jobs that contributed to the maintenance and support of the institution itself. Later on, so-called sheltered workshops, originally attached to the institution, employed the handicapped in light industry.

The exploitation of patients' labor for the maintenance of residential institutions has received a lot of attention in the courts in recent years. Under the heading of "therapy," thousands of residents of institutions have been forced to work without pay at such menial tasks as cleaning, laundering, dishwashing, and housekeeping. (In some instances, residents have even participated in the care of other patients.) In 1970 alone, labor performed by mentally retarded persons confined to institutions was valued at $1.25 million.

All these tasks would have to be performed by regular paid employees if the residents did not complete them. Clearly their work has nothing to do with therapy or the treatment they are supposed to be receiving, and this kind of labor is known as "institutional peonage."

These tasks are reportedly done on a "voluntary" basis, but those who do not cooperate are often punished by a loss of privileges or an increase in medication. In some instances certain work assignments are used as punishments themselves. For example, one class-action suit filed in Illinois in 1970 on behalf of two mentally retarded youths committed to an institution charged that, among other abuses they had been subjected to, the young men had been forced to wash walls for over ten consecutive hours on several occasions.

A number of suits filed over the years have resulted in a series of rulings that have established a right to payment for institution-maintaining labor. Basing their decisions on the Thirteenth Amendment's prohibition against involuntary servitude, the courts have declared that the exploitation of resident labor is unconstitutional. Other rulings have cited the minimum-wage amendments to the 1938 Fair Labor Standards Act. In the *Wyatt* case, discussed in Chapter 4, the court ruled that "patients may voluntarily engage in . . . labor if the labor is compensated in accordance with the minimum wage laws of the Fair Labor Standards Act." The ruling went on to outline the differences between therapeutic and non-therapeutic (and deserving of payment) labor.

For the disabled adult outside the institutional setting the problem is not one of receiving compensation for work done but of finding work at all. Employers have used a number of excuses for their failure to hire the handicapped over the years, all of which have been proven by the facts to be groundless. Among the most popular myths about the disabled employee are:

—His presence will cause the company's insurance rates to soar.
—Costly physical adjustments to the workplace will have to be made to accommodate him.
—He will require special treatment and privileges.
—He will have a negative effect on the company's safety record.
—His work will not be up to standard.
—He will have a high rate of absenteeism.
—He is unlikely to stay with the job.
—The other employees will not accept him.

Let's take a closer look at these false ideas, starting with the first one. First of all, a company's accident insurance rates are not based on who is hired, but on the actual accident experience of the company and the hazards of the industry as a whole. This means that the mere act of hiring a disabled employee does not automatically affect a company's accident-insurance rates. The same holds true for group health plans, pension programs, and other related employee benefit programs. A recent survey of 279 companies conducted by the United States Chamber of Commerce and the National Association of Manufacturers revealed that 90 percent of those companies experienced no effect whatever on insurance costs as a result of hiring disabled employees.

In 1973, E. I. du Pont de Nemours and Company, then America's sixteenth largest company, conducted one of the most extensive studies of handicapped workers to date. Data was gathered on 1,452 of the company's physically disabled employees over an eight-month period. The survey's findings regarding physical adjustments to the workplace were that "most employees require no special work arrangements." Most other companies who employ the handicapped have reported that a minimum of adjustments, such as a lowered workbench or the addition of a ramp, was all that was required.

As for special privileges, James H. Sears, coordinator of industry education at du Pont, had this to say upon completion of the study:

> The disabled [person] wants to be treated as a normal employee. Fellow employees do not consider a parking spot near the plant entrance for a paraplegic in a wheel-

chair to be a misuse of executive privilege. They wouldn't trade places and don't expect the same treatment.

Far from being a risk to his company's safety record, the disabled employee is likely to improve it because he tends to be more safety-conscious than his fellow employees. This is borne out by the du Pont study. It found that 96 percent of du Pont's handicapped workers rated average or better on safety, both on and off the job, than the able-bodied workers. Another survey, conducted by the United States Office of Vocational Rehabilitation based on reports from more than one hundred large corporations, found that the accident rate was lower for the disabled in 57 percent of the companies surveyed; another 41 percent reported that the accident rate was the same for both handicapped and nonhandicapped workers. Only 2 percent of the employers said the accident rate was higher for their disabled employees. In addition, statistics show that the disabled worker is no more likely to be injured or become ill on the job than the nondisabled worker.

Regarding his on-the-job performance, the disabled worker is likely to outperform and outproduce his fellow workers in quality as well as quantity. The United States Office of Vocational Rehabilitation study shows that 24 percent of its respondents reported that the handicapped rated higher than the nonhandicapped in productivity, 66 percent reported that both groups rated about the same, and only 10 percent said that productivity was lower for the handicapped. The du Pont survey's results were similar. It found that 91 percent of its disabled employees performed as well or better than the nondisabled.

It is a fact that the disabled person who is properly trained and placed in the right job usually proves to be more reliable than his nonhandicapped counterparts. He is conscientious and his attendance record tends to be excellent. The du Pont study found that 79 percent of its disabled workers were average or better in attendance than the rest of the du Pont work force. The U.S. Office of Vocational Rehabilitation survey came up with an even better record among the companies it surveyed. Its figures show 55 percent of the companies reporting that their disabled employees have a lower rate of absenteeism, while 40 percent found there was no difference in attendance between the disabled and the nondisabled.

Another good point about the disabled employee is that once he is hired he tends to stay put. He is less likely to "job hop" than his fellow workers, and is thus more likely to save his employer time and money in training and hiring. The du Pont Company found that 93 percent of its disabled workers rated average or better when it came to job stability. The Office of Vocational Rehabilitation discovered that turnover rates were lower for the disabled in 83 percent of the corporations reporting in its survey, and the same for disabled and nondisabled in 16 percent. That left a minimal one percent reporting a higher turnover rate among the disabled.

When it comes to relations between disabled and nondisabled workers, all surveys indicate that once the disabled individual is on the job he is readily accepted by his fellow workers. Any initial suspicion or fear disappears once his fellow workers see that he can do the job, and that he asks for no special favors or unreasonable concessions. In fact, his presence and his eagerness to prove himself equal to his job are probably a boost to general employee morale. As one supervisor said of a severely disabled employee: "He adds pride, makes us all feel good about the place. He is a motivating factor. You take a look at [him] working hard and you want to work up to your own potential—how could we do anything less?"

At least one company has found that it is good business to rehabilitate workers who become disabled on the job. As Paul Ashton, director of the Minnesota Mining and Manufacturing Company's (3-M's) vocational rehabilitation program, explains:

> Funding, hiring and training of a person for a particular job can run into several thousand dollars. When illness, injury, or emotional problems prevent that person from performing a job, the company can lose its investment. And paying insurance costs to a disabled employee instead of paying a salary to a productive one, is a further drain.

Under the program, 3-M employees who become disabled are given whatever assistance they need to return to the jobs they held before they were injured, or are trained to perform new ones. For example, a 3-M shipping clerk who strained his back and was unable to return to the job on a warehouse loading dock that he had held for nineteen years was retrained as a raw materials analyst. Today he is earning more

Disabled workers on the job. (Top: Human Resources Center. Middle: United Cerebral Palsy. Bottom: The President's Committee on Employment of the Handicapped)

than he did as a shipping clerk and feels that he has "a real future" in his new position at 3-M.

All the facts indicate that the average disabled worker has no problem holding a job or performing well in it. His problem is getting the job in the first place, because, even though the record shows that he would be an asset to any business organization, discriminatory hiring practices persist.

Congress has passed a number of laws over the years designed to force employers out of these bad habits. In 1948 the disabled were specifically mentioned for the first time in federal legislation dealing with employment practices. In that year Congress amended the Civil Service Act to prohibit discrimination against the handicapped in federal employment. This piece of legislation was in keeping with the development of a national policy of fair-employment practices and equal-employment opportunity promoted during the administration of President Franklin D. Roosevelt.

The most important piece of federal legislation relating to employment of the disabled enacted to date is the Rehabilitation Act of 1973. Section 504 of that act prohibits discrimination against the handicapped "under any program or activity receiving Federal financial assistance." The regulations for the implementation of Section 504 adopted by the Department of Health, Education, and Welfare in April of 1977 contain provisions relating to employment practices. Under these provisions an employer is expected to make "reasonable accommodations" in the workplace for handicapped employees. In addition, employers are no longer permitted to ask about the nature and extent of a person's disability before he is hired, and no handicapped person can be denied employment on the basis of his handicap, unless it can be demonstrated that his impairment will interfere with his performance on the job.

Section 501 of the Rehabilitation Act requires all federal agencies to adopt a plan of "affirmative action" in the hiring, placement, and advancement of the handicapped. The idea behind this is that the federal government should be a "model" employer setting an example for the rest of the country.

The scope of affirmative action goes far beyond the mere adoption of a policy of nondiscrimination. It means that federal agencies must actively seek qualified disabled applicants to fill jobs that are open; make necessary accommodations for them in the workplace; offer them on-the-job training to assist them in career advancement; and make every effort to see to it that a person who becomes disabled on the job can keep his job, or be assigned to a new one that fits his capabilities.

Section 503 of the Rehabilitation Act extends the affirmative-action requirements to cover all those employers who hold federal contracts in excess of $2,500. This applies to about half of all the businesses in the United States, including virtually all of the leading industries. Any disabled individual who feels he has been discriminated against by such an employer can file a complaint with the Department of Labor, which has been given the responsibility of promptly investigating and resolving all such complaints.

The employment practices of Sections 501, 503, and 504

of the Rehabilitation Act cover just about every major employer in the country. Between 1975 and 1977, 3,500 employment discrimination complaints were filed with the Labor Department. Ironically, the federal government, which is supposed to be a model for other employers in regard to the hiring of the handicapped, has been the object of a great number of complaints. In fact, the number of handicapped federal employees actually declined by 3,500 in the two years following the enactment of the Rehabilitation Act. According to Debby Kaplan, director of the Disability Rights Center in Washington, D.C., which is closely monitoring the federal government's compliance with Section 501 of the Rehabilitation Act, "They [people in government] don't take the law seriously."

Numerous court actions citing violations of the Rehabilitation Act, as well as violations of the due-process and equal-protection rights of the Constitution, have also been brought by handicapped individuals denied employment.

In 1974, for example, Michael P. Zorick of Los Angeles, an amateur wrestler, applied to the Clay County School Board in Florida for a job as a physical-education teacher and was hired over the phone. But when the school board found out that Mr. Zorick was blind, the job offer was withdrawn. Mr. Zorick brought suit against the school board, and in October of 1977 Circuit Court Judge Susan Black ruled that the board was obliged to hire Mr. Zorick and allow him to "demonstrate whether he can satisfactorily perform the work of a physical education teacher." Litigation of this sort is likely to increase, unless employers' attitudes fall in line with the new law.

The Right to Employment and Compensation

In addition to regulations regarding employment practices, the Rehabilitation Act has several provisions that deal with vocational training and rehabilitation. Every state has some kind of vocational rehabilitation agency, presumably designed to give the handicapped individualized programs of counseling, education, training, and financial assistance as needed in preparation for future employment. The Rehabilitation Act has set certain guidelines for state vocational rehabilitation programs regarding eligibility for services, and so on, and those states that fail to comply with these guidelines are liable to lose federal funding.

In spite of these regulations, a great deal of discrimination occurs within the vocational rehabilitation programs themselves. Most of these agencies receive federal funding based on the number of clients they actually place in jobs. This has led to the widespread practice known as "creaming" in state agencies. This means that agencies often extend their aid only to the most mildly disabled and, therefore, those most likely to succeed in finding employment. In some instances, people who have "disabilities" no worse than occasional insomnia or headaches have been given assistance. These abuses are clearly in violation of the law, which was designed to help the most severely disabled, the ones who have the most difficulty securing permanent employment.

Further discrimination occurs within the agencies when it comes to the type of training offered and job placement recommended to the severely disabled. Severely disabled people seeking counseling and training are often discouraged from pursuing job goals agency professionals consider "unrealistic." In some cases this kind of advice may be appropriate, but all too often it is based on the counselor's limited view of his client, rather than the client's real potential. Certain employment stereotypes are rigidly adhered to in these agencies. For instance, the retarded are considered good for boring, repetitive assembly-line type work, blind people are good at memory work, and so on. It is very difficult for disabled individuals to break out of these stereotypes.

In addition, any training the severely disabled are likely to receive under the guidance of a vocational rehabilitation agency is usually geared toward permanent employment in a sheltered workshop. For some, employment in the sheltered setting is the best choice, but it should never be regarded as a dead end or as a last stop on the employment ladder. Rather, it should be viewed as another step in vocational training that will bring the disabled worker closer to his ultimate goal—employment in a normal setting.

At the very least, workers in a sheltered setting should receive payment that is equal to the prevailing wage in industry for the kind of work they are doing. Quite often wages in the sheltered workshop are well below the industrial standard, although worker performance is up to industry requirements. Disabled employees in a sheltered workshop in Clinton, Iowa, recently became the first such group to unionize. It is hoped that this kind of action will lead to improved conditions for the worker in the sheltered setting.

Perhaps if state as well as private or voluntary agencies that are supposed to help the handicapped in their quest for employment had more disabled employees on their staffs, the situation would improve. So far, however, these agencies have proven notoriously discriminatory in their own hiring practices. When Edward Koch, Mayor of New York City, was a United States congressman, he conducted a survey of nine voluntary health organizations and found that out of a total of 382 persons employed by the five agencies that responded only 23 were disabled in any way. Mayor Koch had this to say about his findings:

> there is no excuse for the discriminatory hiring practices of the voluntary agencies, which have been created to serve the handicapped. The handicapped individual should be the usual employee of these agencies and the non-handicapped should be the exception.

Employees at the office of The President's Committee on Employment of the Handicapped participate in a class in sign language to facilitate their communication with deaf and hearing-impaired people. (The President's Committee on Employment of the Handicapped)

COMPENSATION

Galen, the Greek philosopher and physician, once said: "Employment is nature's best physician." While this statement may be true, the physically disabled often need employment for reasons that are more practical than therapeutic.

All of us—aside from the fortunate few who are born to wealth—depend on some kind of employment to sustain ourselves financially. The physical needs of the disabled often extend way beyond the basics of food, clothing, and shelter. They can include health care, medication, physical therapy, prosthetic devices, rehabilitative aids, attendant care, and many other life-support necessities, all of which are quite costly. And these expenses do not ordinarily occur on a one-time basis. They represent a constant, lifelong drain on the disabled individual's finances, and, depending on the nature of the disability and the rate of monetary inflation, these costs are likely to increase as time goes on.

Given these facts, it would be safe to assume that the severely disabled person's income needs are more substantial than the average nonhandicapped person's. Even if every disabled person was permanently employed at a decent wage —a condition the majority of the disabled do not even come close to meeting at this time—they would probably not be earning enough to cover all their expenses. And one cannot overlook those extreme cases in which a person's disability is so severe that it prevents him from doing any kind of work at all, either temporarily or for a lifetime.

Over the years the federal and state governments have experimented with a number of different programs designed to supplement the income of the disabled and their families. These programs of "income maintenance," as they are called, have never been satisfactory in their scope and handling of the complex problem. The regulations governing them have been complicated and the selection of recipients of funds has often appeared arbitrary.

In January 1974, a new federal program of Supplemental Security Income (SSI), intended to replace all the other welfare-type programs for the elderly, blind, and physically disabled, was introduced. Under this program, the federal government guarantees a minimum income to all those disabled who have no other totally sufficient source of income.

This program is supposed to cover basic living expenses such as food, clothing, and housing. It is not intended to cover the cost of medical care. Medicare and Medicaid payments are supposed to meet those needs.

Under the SSI program, the states are supposed to work in a partnership with the federal government by supplementing the basic SSI payments with state funds. So far thirty-eight states and the District of Columbia have programs designed to supplement SSI.

Like its predecessors, SSI is not without its flaws. Payments are low (the current maximum for a single person is $177.80 per month, for couples $266.70), and the states have not always been forthcoming with their supplemental payments. In addition, establishing eligibility can be a difficult, delay-ridden, and ultimately futile process. The number of lawsuits involving disability benefits doubled between 1973 and 1977, and they are expected to increase at a rate of 25 percent or more a year.

The benefit system can also discriminate against those who work. Tom Clancy, a $21,000-a-year computer program analyst for New York University, is almost totally paralyzed in the arms and legs as a result of polio. He must sleep with a respirator, is dependent on other special equipment, and is in need of almost constant attendance. But because he earns over $200 a month, he is not eligible for supplemental aid from the city, and he is running into debt trying to pay for everything on his own.

"They've made it clear," Mr. Clancy says, "that if only I stop trying, they'll take care of everything. If I would agree to give up my job, become totally indigent and totally dependent on the city, I'd qualify for maximum disability benefits, twenty-four-hour care, a disability pension from the University, and I'd also qualify for subsidized rent and food. I'd come close to receiving the equivalent of twenty five thousand dollars a year tax free.

"I have no intention of doing it. I kind of like the idea of paying taxes, my insurance, and my pension. I'll go down the drain before I give up my job."

Another approach to easing the financial burden of disability is through the adjustment of our income-tax laws. At present there is a provision in the United States Tax Code that allows individuals who maintain a household to deduct expenses for household services and attendant care for handicapped dependents. Another provision allows a standard exemption of $750 for those who are blind.

These kinds of tax credits are discriminatory. If a parent, spouse, or guardian can deduct expenses for the care of disabled dependents, why shouldn't the disabled be allowed to deduct their own special expenses? And if the blind are entitled to a tax exemption, why not all those who suffer from a physical disability? Clearly some more equitable system of tax credits or adjustments based on individual income and physical requirements needs to be established.

Tax deductions, wage supplements, SSI, Medicaid, disability benefits, and so on, are not meant to take the place of real earned income. They are merely income aids that are of a temporary or stop-gap nature. None of them, either alone or in a combination, can fully sustain the disabled individual who is dependent on them.

A number of bills calling for a variety of tax adjustments and wage supplements for the disabled are currently pending in the United States Congress. These include provisions for the deduction of employment-related expenses paid or incurred by disabled individuals, deductions for special expenses paid for medical care of disabled taxpayers or dependents, deduction without limitation of all medical expenses of the disabled, and wage supplements for disabled employees in sheltered workshops.

There is still much that needs to be done if disabled Americans are ever to achieve a decent standard of living. An all-out nationwide push for affirmative action in hiring, placement, and advancement of the disabled is needed. Vocational rehabilitation services must be restructured so that the disabled are assisted according to their need, with the most severely disabled receiving priority attention. In addition, increased cooperation between vocational rehabilitation agencies and state employment services should be fostered. And these services should not wait for the disabled to come to them. They should initiate a policy of seeking out those most in need of assistance. The boost the addition of thousands of productive individuals to the American work force would give our economy should be incentive enough to activate these reforms.

Those who are not able to earn an adequate living, or are too disabled to work at all, should not be penalized for their lack of productivity. They have just as much right to a decent life as the next person and ideally should be guaranteed an income sufficient for their needs. Existing tax laws, medical-assistance, wage-supplement, and income-maintenance programs, need to be revamped to better serve the severely disabled.

7

The Right to a Barrier-Free Environment

The handicapped individual has the right to barrier-free public facilities which include buildings, mass . . . transportation services and social, recreational and entertainment facilities.

—A BILL OF RIGHTS FOR THE HANDICAPPED,
United Cerebral Palsy Associations

A typical day in the life of the average adult American probably goes something like this:

Morning: He or she wakes up. Gets out of bed. Enters the bathroom. Uses the toilet. Washes. Shaves or puts on makeup. Gets dressed. Has a cup of coffee. Leaves the house. Heads to work via car or public transportation.

At Work: Walks up steps to office or plant. Goes through door. Rides elevator. Sits down at desk or workbench. Works until it's time to break for lunch. Has a bite to eat in the company cafeteria. Goes out to do some errands: shops, stops at the post office, goes to the bank, etc. Maybe makes a phone call, using a public phone. Has a drink from a water fountain. Uses the restroom. Goes back to work.

After Work: Returns home. Fixes dinner. Goes out for an evening with friends or to see a movie. Or maybe stays home and plans the weekend—a baseball game on Saturday, church on Sunday.

Does this sound like a fairly average day? It may even seem a little dull because it has been stripped down to its most basic elements. Only the most ordinary activities that most of us take for granted have been included.

Now let's take a look at what happens when a person with a disability—a paraplegic confined to a wheelchair—proceeds through a typical day.

Morning: Upon waking, he faces the problem of getting up from a conventional bed and into his wheelchair. Depending upon the degree of his impairment, he may not be able to accomplish this task unassisted.

Once in his chair he will most likely have to make a perilous journey down a narrow hallway in order to get to the bathroom. Again he will need assistance because he probably won't be able to get his wheelchair through the door—the standard doorway in the typical American home is too narrow to accommodate the standard wheelchair.

In the bathroom, he will undoubtedly have trouble using the toilet facilities because there is nothing for him to grab onto to steady himself as he moves from wheelchair to toilet seat. He will have the same kind of difficulty getting into the average shower or tub.

Even if he could reach the light switch over his head to turn on the bathroom lights, he probably wouldn't be able to shave anyway because the bathroom mirror has been placed too high for him to see anything but the top of his head. Brushing his teeth will also be a problem, because there will be no room for his legs under the sink, and he won't be able to reach the water faucet.

Getting dressed is another problem because he won't be able to reach the clothing hung over his head in the closet.

When he gets to the kitchen, cabinets that are out of his reach and a stove top that is chest-high will keep him from making his cup of coffee.

Getting to work presents a whole other set of problems. If he is fortunate enough to be able to afford a car that has been specially altered to suit his needs, he won't have too much trouble getting to his job. He might be late for work, however, if he doesn't allow enough time for the tasks of getting himself into the car and storing his wheelchair in the back seat. Getting out at the other end will be equally time consuming, especially if he is forced to park some distance from the plant or office entrance.

If he has to rely on public transportation, in all but a very few locations in this country, he may as well forget about going to work at all. The standard bus, subway, or rail system cannot accommodate his wheelchair.

At Work: At his place of work he will most likely be confronted with a flight of steps leading up to the building's entrance. Steps are absolutely impossible to negotiate in a wheelchair.

If his company has installed a ramp, he will be able to wheel his way to the entrance, but he will still have to get through the front door. A revolving door is obviously out of the question for a person in a wheelchair. He may be able to handle the heavy push-pull type door. If he possesses extraordinary agility and strength, he may be able to get it open and keep it open with one arm while he uses his other hand to maneuver his bulky chair inside.

If he takes an elevator, however, he may not have enough room inside the car to turn his wheelchair around so that he can face the floor buttons. If he is able to turn around, the chances are that the floor buttons will be out of his reach.

When he's finally made it to his office or work site, he's going to have trouble trying to wheel his chair under his desk (too low) or reach the tools on his workbench (too high).

At lunchtime, let's hope he's had the foresight to bring a sandwich from home (if he is able to get around in his kitchen to make a sandwich) because there is no way he is going to make it through the narrow cafeteria line, juggling a trayful of food on his knees. He may as well forget the idea of doing any errands during his lunch hour. Flights of stairs and revolving doors at the bank, post office, and most commercial buildings will probably send him back to the office early. That phone call will also have to wait, because he cannot reach the dial on the public phone in the company lobby. If he's thirsty, too bad, because he can't fit his chair under the water fountain or reach the handle. A trip to the rest room will prove equally futile, because the stalls are likely to be too narrow for his chair to fit through. He will need assistance.

After Work: After the frustrating day he's had, he will again have to face a difficult trip home and more difficulties once he gets there. Hungry for a hot meal, he will again face the familiar and discouraging obstacles in his kitchen. He might consider going out for the evening. But where? A restaurant? The movies? They have no place for a person in a wheelchair.

And what about the weekend? A baseball game and even church are out. There is no place to put him and his wheelchair.

Clearly, a "typical" day isn't so typical when it is experienced by a person with a physical disability. So many of the routine tasks and activities most of us perform without even thinking present tremendous obstacles that must be dealt with each day by a large number of disabled individuals. For some, these recurring hurdles prove impossible to overcome. What is for most of us a familiar, even friendly world, is for the severely disabled individual a strange and hostile environment.

As one man in a wheelchair describes his experience:

Society in general is ill-equipped to deal with me. In the last fifteen years, my wheelchair and I have been declared a fire hazard in several theaters. I have been served meals in separate dining areas of restaurants since, as the owners were quick to point out, I might upset the other customers and lessen their enjoyment of the meal. On several occasions I have been very nearly hit by traffic as I worked my way across the street hoping to find a ramp or driveway onto the sidewalk on the other side.

Our journey through a day in the life of a paraplegic (imagine for yourself the kinds of difficulties people with other types of disabilities must confront) should make one thing quite clear: a disabled person's ability to negotiate our man-made environment directly affects his or her ability to pursue any other activity in which he might be interested. A right to education is meaningless if a person cannot get up the schoolhouse steps, or through the classroom door. A right to equal-opportunity employment cannot help if there is no way of getting to a job, or of fitting behind the office desk. A right to the prevention and alleviation of the daily problems associated with physical disability is ridiculous if one is faced with an environment that is an obstacle course. Even a right to treatment becomes impossible to enforce when so many hospital settings are not accessible to the severely disabled yet still mobile patient.

What ultimately makes it all so absurd, though, is the fact that it doesn't have to be this way at all. We have largely created the environment in which we live. We have chosen to construct it in such a way as to alienate the disabled. Thus, it isn't any physical impairment that prevents a disabled person from moving about the world freely so much as it is the obstacles that have been built into our environment. If you follow this line of reasoning to its logical conclusion it becomes apparent that people rather than nature are really responsible for most "handicaps." One student of design has explained the situation in the following way:

> People are often handicapped not so much by their afflictions as by the design of products they have to deal with daily. When a person cannot open a door because limited twisting motion in his wrist prevents him from

turning the knob, our culture says *he* is handicapped. But redesign the door knob so it requires no twisting motion, and he opens it easily. The handicap is no more. So the question arises: Which really had the handicap, the person or the door?

In response to the growing outcry of the disabled over the barriers to their functioning that exist in our society, American designers, architects, planners, and public officials have begun to rethink their approach to the creation of our man-made environment. Traditionally, buildings and products have all been constructed with the average person and normal circumstances in mind. As we have seen, however, this kind of thinking has led to a situation that is nothing short of intolerable for the disabled. There are a number of new approaches to the problem that could improve the quality of life for all of us, able-bodied and disabled alike. Many designers have come to realize that what is good in design for the disabled often proves to be better for the able-bodied as well. Taking the door handle mentioned by the designer quoted above as an example, architect Stephen Klimet has concluded ". . . a door handle requiring downward pressure instead of a twisting motion will help not only those with loss of hand function but all able-bodied people, especially those with loads."

There are many other instances. Ramps are easier for everyone to negotiate than steps. The mother pushing a baby carriage or stroller would readily agree with that. Wider doors are an asset in times of emergency, such as fire.

As architect James F. Hilleary has stated:

The truth is that there is no clearly defined separation between the well and the infirm and that in our time many of those considered well suffer some infirmity. The old idea that a barrier-free architecture was catering to a minority is no longer valid.

In 1959 the President's Committee on Employment of the Handicapped in conjunction with the National Easter Seal Society for Crippled Children and Adults and a number of other public and private agencies launched the first nationwide campaign to eliminate architectural barriers. A direct result of this collaboration was the development of a document known as *Specifications for Making Buildings and Facilities Accessible to, and Usable by, the Physically Handicapped.* Published in 1961 by the American National Standards Institute (ANSI), Standard 117.1—as the document is known—outlines minimum requirements for accommodation of the disabled in the construction of public buildings. Since the ANSI standard first appeared, awareness of the problem and how to deal with it has grown. The standard is currently being revised and expanded.

In 1965 the United States Congress directly addressed the issue of architectural barriers in public buildings for the first time by amending the Vocational Rehabilitation Act to establish the National Commission on Architectural Barriers to the Rehabilitation of the Handicapped. The commission was to study the problem and propose ways of dealing with it.

The Right to Barrier-Free Environment

In 1967 the commission recommended that Congress enact legislation requiring accessibility for the handicapped in all buildings leased, owned, or constructed with federal funds. The Congress responded with the Architectural Barriers Act of 1968 (PL 90-480), which states: "Any building constructed or leased in whole or in part with federal funds must be made accessible to and usable by the physically handicapped." The act pertained to buildings intended for public use and specifically excluded military installations and privately constructed housing.

Section 502 of the 1973 Rehabilitation Act provided for the establishment of the Architectural Barriers and Transportation Compliance Board. The board was given the power to "conduct investigations, hold public hearings and issue such orders as it deems necessary to insure compliance with the standards of accessibility" established under the Architectural Barriers Act of 1968. Sections 501, 503, and 504 of the Rehabilitation Act, discussed in Chapter 6, cover the affirmative-action aspects of architectural accessibility.

By 1974 all fifty states and the District of Columbia had enacted legislation that required all newly constructed public buildings to be accessible to the disabled. Most such legislation, whether it be federal or state, has been limited in two important areas: scope and enforceability.

The federal laws apply only to buildings and facilities that are presently under construction or are to be constructed in the future. That means that the thousands of inaccessible public buildings that were built in the past and still stand today are not covered by legislation. Furthermore, both state and federal legislation leave a lot of room for individual interpretation of just what making a building accessible involves. Each agency embarking on a building project is responsible only to itself for setting standards and, as a result, many new public buildings do not meet even minimum ANSI standards. Inadequate funding also prevents investigations and on-site inspections of construction to determine compliance with the law and there exists no specifically enforceable penalty for noncompliance.

A 1975 Report to the Congress by the comptroller general of the United States based on inspections of 314 federally financed buildings constructed, altered, or leased since the enactment of the Architectural Barriers Act of 1968 highlighted the inadequacies of such legislation as it exists. The General Accounting Office, responsible for conducting the inspections, found that *none* of the buildings inspected was completely free of barriers, and that the buildings being designed and constructed were only slightly more free from barriers than buildings designed and constructed immediately after passage of the 1968 Act. The report cited the permissiveness of the act's language and its lack of specificity for this widespread failure in compliance. The report called on Congress to clarify the act.

Congress subsequently amended the Architectural Barriers Act in 1976, using more forceful language and including the United States Postal Service, previously exempt, in its coverage. It is too early to tell if the amended act will be more effective than it was in its original form.

While the Congress has been busy working out its stance on the issue of architectural barriers in public buildings, a number of disabled individuals have taken the issue to the courts. The mere act of physically trying to bring suit in court has turned out in many cases to be a graphic illustration of the problem of accessibility, because many buildings that house courts have architectural barriers that prevent plaintiffs from even entering them. This is a clear violation of a citizen's First Amendment right to petition his or her government for "a redress of grievances." If the disabled are prevented from entering the buildings where the business of government is conducted, how can they successfully petition?

In 1972 an attorney who was confined to a wheelchair and unable to enter county buildings in Cleveland that contained courtrooms, filed a class-action suit against the county of Cuyahoga in Ohio. In the case of *Friedman v. County of Cuyahoga,* the plaintiff argued that such barriers amounted to a violation of the constitutional right to petition guaranteed in the First Amendment, and the right to equal protection, the right to freedom of movement, and the right to equal opportunity guaranteed in the Fourteenth Amendment. A judicially approved consent decree was reached under which the county promised to insure accessibility to all county-owned buildings and to see to it that all future construction would be accessible.

Another constitutional issue being raised in the courts with regard to architectural barriers in public buildings is the right to vote. Many disabled Americans are unable to register to vote or enter polling places because of architectural barriers. In the case of *Selph, et al. v. Council of the City of Los Angeles, et al.,* a 1974 class-action suit filed on behalf of disabled individuals who were unable to enter polling places, the plaintiff argued that this kind of obstruction was a clear violation of the constitutional right to vote.

In 1975 the district court ruled against the plaintiff, declaring: ". . . a handicapped person has a Constitutional right to vote, but he has no right to insist that city officials modify all polling places within the city so as to eliminate architectural barriers." The judge suggested the disabled use the absentee ballot as an alternative.

This case is now on appeal with the plaintiff maintaining that inaccessible polling places result in the total disenfranchisement of the disabled voter. The plaintiff is arguing that the absentee ballot is not an alternative because a disabled person often has no way of knowing whether his polling place is accessible or not until Election Day, when it is too late to file an absentee ballot. Furthermore, forcing the disabled to use the lengthy and often confusing absentee-voting procedure segregates, stigmatizes, discourages, and often eliminates the handicapped voter altogether.

Cases such as the two discussed above are likely to become more common unless the states and the federal government come up with a viable solution to the problem of architectural barriers in public buildings.

One of the biggest barriers to the free movement of the handicapped in American society is the lack of accessible public transportation. Most buses, subways, trains, planes, and transportation terminals remain inaccessible to a great many of the severely disabled.

In this jet age of rapid movement from one location to

another, nothing so isolates the disabled from the mainstream of activity than the inaccessibility of the various
modes of public transportation. A disabled person cannot
work if he is prevented from using transportation to get to
his job. He cannot have a social life if he cannot get around
to see his friends, or make new ones. He cannot enjoy the
world of the arts, sports, and other public or cultural events
if he cannot go to them.

The federal government has jurisdiction over mass transit
and interstate transportation systems. Congressional legislation to date, however, concerning the mobility of the handicapped, has contained little more than policy statements, or
statements of intent to research the problem of architectural
barriers in public transportation.

Section 16a of the Urban Mass Transportation Act of 1964
as amended in 1970 states that it is

> the national policy that elderly and handicapped per-
> sons have the same right as other persons to utilize mass
> transportation facilities and services; that special efforts
> shall be made in the planning and design of mass trans-
> portation facilities and services so that the availability
> to elderly and handicapped persons of mass transporta-
> tion which they can effectively utilize will be assured;
> and that all Federal programs offering assistance in the
> field of mass transportation . . . should contain provi-
> sions implementing this policy.

This statement of "national policy" can be interpreted in a variety of ways depending on where you
happen to stand on the issue.

In 1975 Senators Frank Church, John Tunney, and Harrison Williams introduced legislation in the Senate known as the National Mass Transit Act of 1975. This act would assure that all federally assisted transit facilities would be designed so as not to discriminate against what the senators call "the nation's forgotten minority—the millions of physically handicapped." The act has yet to be passed.

At the center of this controversy over the accessibility of mass transit are the nation's bus and subway systems. In 1971 the Urban Mass Transportation Administration (UMTA) launched a program that was to produce a design for a "bus of the future" known as the "Transbus." What was called for, at the very least, was a design for a low-floor bus with a single step that could be lowered to accommodate the elderly or infirm, a ramp that could extend to the curb, a wide door, and space inside to accommodate wheelchairs.

After spending $27 million and five years on the development of a design, the UMTA settled on a prototype bus that comes nowhere near meeting the needs of the severely disabled. This model has been designated the official recipient of federal subsidization in spite of the fact that several motor companies have developed model buses that more closely fit the requirements of the disabled.

These buses would indeed be more costly to make, but it has been estimated that the potential profits to be made from increased disabled ridership—13,300,000 Americans are presently unable to use any kind of bus now in service—would offset the expense, and even decrease present public-transit operating costs from 4 to 10 percent. These figures do not even take into consideration the long-range economic benefits that would result from the increased employment of handicapped people who remain "homebound" because of their inability to use the present system.

The UMTA's slowness in implementing regulations that would put an end to barriers in public transportation has prompted a number of lawsuits. The most important case to be brought in the courts to date, *Washington Urban League, Inc., et al. v. Washington Metropolitan Area Transit Authority, Inc.,* resulted in a 1973 court injunction that prohibited the new Metro subway from operating until all its facilities were made accessible to the handicapped. The inaccessible Gallery Place Station on the line remained closed three years after the injunction in spite of efforts of local businesses to have it reopened.

Several other similar cases pending throughout the country cite violations of the Urban Mass Transportation Act's Section 16a, Section 504 of the Rehabilitation Act, the Architectural Barriers Act of 1968, and the constitutional principles safeguarding freedom of movement and equal protection.

The railways and airlines, which are notorious for their discriminatory practices in dealing with the disabled traveler, are the next likely targets for this kind of judicial attack.

On July 5, 1978, over a thousand blind demonstrators marched in front of the Offices of the Federal Aviation Administration in Washington, D.C., carrying signs reading "Fly Me, Cane and All." They were protesting safety regulations requiring them to stow their canes during flight. They argue that passengers carrying tennis rackets and umbrellas are allowed to keep them under their seats and that the regulations discriminate against them. A suit has been filed in the United States Court of Appeals for the District of Columbia calling for the removal of this regulation.

The problem of environmental barriers does not end with government buildings and public transportation. It reaches into the private sector and affects every aspect of the disabled person's life.

Shelter is one of the basic needs of life, but there is very little adequate housing being designed for the disabled in this country. Most conventional homes are designed for the average family and are not readily adaptable to the needs of the disabled.

Remember our paraplegic friend—the one we followed through a "typical" day at the opening of this chapter? He

The placement of this light switch exemplifies the need for thoughtful design of ordinary facilities for the use of the disabled. (Eastern Paralyzed Veterans Association)

The facilities of this model mobile home are completely accessible to the disabled. (National Easter Seal Society for Crippled Children and Adults, Inc.)

had difficulty getting through the narrow halls and doorways of his home and using the bathroom and kitchen. Even turning on a light switch and getting out the front door were major problems.

Most such obstacles could very easily be designed out of housing altogether, or housing that is readily adaptable to the needs of the disabled could be created. Adaptable housing would in fact benefit all homeowners, because it could be easily adjusted to suit their changing needs over the years. As Larry Kirk, a federal housing official who is himself a double amputee observed: "If you're going to spend twenty or thirty years paying for a home, it's a good idea to invest in one you can continue to live in regardless of what happens to you."

The housing industry is unlikely to adopt such radical changes in design criteria, unless it has some kind of immediate economic incentive or governmental pressure to do so. So far the only such incentive has been the availability of government loans and mortgages for housing constructed specifically for the handicapped. This is hardly enough to encourage the creation of a universal housing standard that will benefit all Americans.

It should be quite clear from our discussion so far in this chapter that the idea of venturing out into our man-made environment is enough to give the disabled individual reason to pause. It is a largely unrewarding, frustrating, and often dangerous undertaking. There are, however, a number of oases in our generally hostile environment. There are people in many localities who have taken the time to fashion environments that are hospitable to both the able-bodied and the disabled. Their achievements and thoughtfulness deserve mention because they are proof of the feasibility of creating an environment that is nearly barrier free.

The city of Binghamton, New York, for example, has come up with a bold new design that will eventually reshape its entire downtown area. Under the master plan, government buildings, commercial establishments, cultural and sports facilities, parking garages, and social services will all be linked together by an elevated bridge system exclusively designated for pedestrian traffic. The entire system will be barrier-free, and provide access to all buildings connected by it. If the entire plan is completed as designed—and much of it has already been constructed—Binghamton will become the first city with a downtown area that is totally accessible to the disabled.

Shown here is an area of downtown Binghamton, New York, that has an elevated bridge system for pedestrians. The entire system is barrier-free and provides access to all the buildings it connects. (Binghamton Community Development Department)

California is a leader among the states in the amount of attention it gives to the needs of its disabled citizens. It has earned this distinction largely through the efforts of an especially well-organized and active disabled population, a high concentration of concerned professionals, and a generally responsive state government that has enacted and enforced model legislation in the area of disabled rights.

One of California's most striking successes has been its promotion of accessible public transportation. The new San Francisco Bay Area Rapid Transit (BART) has been designed so as to be completely accessible to the disabled. All stations have elevators that can accommodate wheelchairs, and train doors are wide enough to fit two wheelchairs at a time.

The trains of San Francisco's Bay Area Rapid Transit system have doors wide enough to accommodate two wheelchairs at a time. (Bay Area Rapid Transit District)

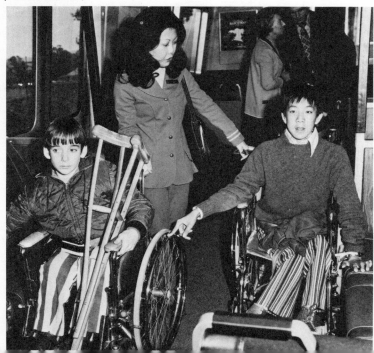

The Right to Barrier-Free Environment

Southern California Rapid Transit in Los Angeles has been trying for years to purchase the fully accessible "bus of the future," which was being developed by UMTA. When UMTA settled on another less-accessible model of the Transbus, Los Angeles immediately ordered two hundred of the new buses, viewing the purchase as an interim measure until a fully accessible bus is on the market.

In the area of accessible recreational facilities, Los Angeles County is again in the forefront. Its Department of Parks and Recreation was among the first such agencies in the nation to make the facilities of its parks completely accessible. Over a two-year period it managed to renovate and remove barriers in all eighty-nine of its parks.

It is usually the case in any discussion of architectural barriers that attention is focused primarily on the needs of the wheelchair-bound. Their particular plight is highly visible to the rest of us. A person in a wheelchair stranded at the foot of a flight of stairs is one of the most poignant and often used illustrations of the problem of environmental barriers.

But there are individuals with other types of disabilities, particularly sensory disabilities, such as hearing or visual impairment, who are confronted with a different but no less difficult set of obstacles to overcome. Their special needs should not be overlooked in the development of standards and policies affecting the removal of environmental barriers.

There are a number of programs and facilities in existence that are models of what a little thoughtfulness and innovative design can do to alleviate their particular difficulties.

The designers of the Vacation Camp for the Blind in

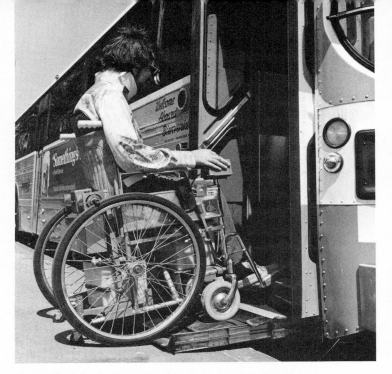

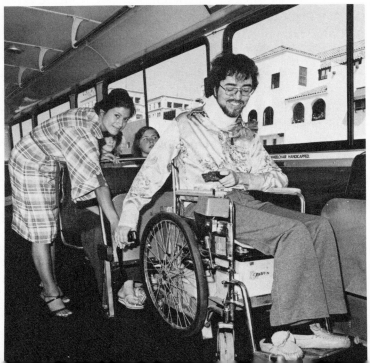

Spring Valley, New York, for example, have created an environment that is totally hospitable for the blind vacationer. The designers of the camp extended their plan far beyond the mere removal of obstacles and barriers. In doing so, they entered another dimension in designing for the disabled. The environment at the Vacation Camp for the Blind is not only barrier-free, it is life-enhancing.

Claude Samton, the designer of the camp, believes that

Architecture can work for the blind as it does for the seeing. It can appeal to their sense of beauty—which they have as much as the seeing.

If you limit architecture to the seeing, you limit both architecture and the blind. You can create an architecture for the blind and it can be more than protective devices like bars at the tops of stairways. But first of all it has to work as does any kind of architecture. By using sounds, smells and special textures, we can design buildings and landscape to guide and liberate the blind in the same way structures erected for the eye do for the seeing.

Each sense of the blind vacationer is brought into play to give him a feeling of place. A fountain at the entrance to the camp is a sensory cue indicating location, as are other strategically placed "sound sculptures"—seashells hung from strings, bamboo poles, and metal rods that make noise as the wind blows through them—fragrant plants, varied ground surfaces, and textures.

The Southern California Rapid Transit in Los Angeles has equipped its buses with lifts at the doors (top) and special seating areas inside (bottom) for the wheelchair handicapped. (Southern California Rapid Transit District)

The Vacation Camp for the Blind is a highly specialized environment that would be impossible to duplicate in the everyday world. Several of the design techniques employed there, however, particularly the use of varied textures and surfaces as place indicators, could be adapted for general use. For example, the planners of the new Illinois Regional Library for the Blind and Physically Handicapped in Chicago used texture, color, and design to create an attractive environment that serves the special needs of the disabled. Bright colors on the outside walls are visually appealing to those with limited vision. Inside, lowered windows allow people in wheelchairs to enjoy the view, while a studded rubber tile floor prevents slipping. Book delivery areas are arranged along one wall, to make it easier for the blind to orient themselves, and there is ample room for wheelchairs to maneuver.

Similar sensory indicators such as flashing lights in place of doorbells and vibrating bells in place of fire alarms have been developed to assist the hearing-impaired to maneuver in their environment.

The model programs discussed here indicate that the technology and the design capability now exist to construct buildings and products that are usable for everyone. The usual argument for not considering the disabled in architectural design and planning is the economic one. But a majority of the studies conducted on this problem so far suggest that the additional costs of planning and building with the disabled in mind are limited. The comptroller general's 1975 report to the Congress has this to say about costs:

Government, private contractor, and design personnel agree that the cost of accessibility features is negligible when such items are incorporated in the design phase; sometimes they may even result in cost savings. In addition, although the cost of altering existing inaccessible buildings is more than that of initial barrier-free construction, it is relatively small when compared to the total construction cost.

A 1967 study conducted by the National League of Cities found that the cost of eliminating barriers at the initial design stage was well below 1 percent of total production costs for a majority of the buildings surveyed. Estimates for altering buildings after they have been constructed, according to the comptroller general's report, range from .06 percent to 2.4 percent of the total project cost.

Construction costs have been further offset by a provision in the Tax Reform Act of 1976 that allows for the deduction of the cost of removing architectural or transportational barriers for the elderly or the handicapped from taxes. (The deduction is limited to $25,000 a year.) In addition, federal loans are available for the elimination of barriers in many instances.

Even when the costs of removing barriers seem high, one must agree with the Department of Health, Education, and Welfare's handbook, *Design of Barrier-Free Facilities,* which states: "The value to society of having the disabled population more fully independent and usefully employed outweighs the cost of making facilities accessible."

*   *   *

In 1957 President Eisenhower was to present an award to the handicapped American of the year. When the recipient of the award arrived in Washington, D.C., for the ceremonies, he was unable to get into the building where they were being held. The man was in a wheelchair, and he was confronted with insurmountable architectural barriers. He finally had to be lifted up several flights of stairs by two marines.

Today many public buildings in our nation's capital remain inaccessible to the disabled. A sit-in at the Lincoln Memorial in 1973 protested that facility's inaccessibility. The list includes the Capitol building itself. When he was a congressman, Edward I. Koch had this to say about what he calls an "intolerable situation": "The handicapped face enough barriers in their day-to-day lives. How long must they now wait for equal access to our nation's Capitol?"

The fact that the Capitol remains inaccessible to the physically disabled after all the studies, mandates, and statements of "national policy" that have been issued over the years is illustrative of what really is at the heart of the problem of environmental barriers. The real problem is not the environmental barriers themselves so much as the attitudinal barriers within the minds of most Americans that allow this kind of situation to persist.

The only way to alleviate the situation is to educate Americans, particularly those responsible for the creation as well as the removal of barriers—architects, builders, contractors, planners, product manufacturers, policymakers—to be more

110

aware of and sensitive to the physical needs of the disabled. These attitudinal barriers must be attacked and corrected at their source before any substantial progress can be made toward the removal of the environmental barriers our indifference has created.

The Right to Choose

*The handicapped person has the right to function indepen-
dently in any way in which he is able to act on his own and
to obtain the assistance he may need to assure mobility, communication and daily living activities; to live how and where
he chooses and to enjoy residential accommodations which
meet his needs if he cannot function in conventional housing.*

—A BILL OF RIGHTS FOR THE HANDICAPPED,
United Cerebral Palsy Associations

The right to be able to lead one's own life in the way one
chooses is something the majority of Americans take for
granted. The pursuit of this right is what brought to this
country many of our ancestors, who had been denied religious, political, and individual freedom in their European
homelands.

The Declaration of Independence is much more than a
statement of our Founding Fathers' desire to sever their
connection with their distant masters. Its very title—Declaration of *Independence*—proclaims the most essential quality of what has come to be known as the distinctively Ameri-

112

can character. Independence, personal freedom, individual liberty, these are the life blood of this nation. The spirit of independence, along with the democratic principle of equality, is what makes the United States and its people unique.

It is ironic, however, to find in a country devoted to the ideals of freedom and independence so many people who are forced to live a life characterized by the restraint of freedom and by dependence, but this is precisely the predicament in which the physically disabled and mentally retarded have found themselves throughout our nation's history.

Just as the American patriots sought to free themselves from their colonial overseers two hundred years ago, the disabled today are seeking independence from an oppressive social system that keeps them from controlling their own lives. Being able to make one's own decisions about where and with whom one will live, where one will go to school, what kind of career one will pursue, and the kinds of leisure activities one will engage in, without interference, are what personal independence is all about.

Until quite recently most severely disabled persons, particularly the mentally retarded and multiply handicapped, were routinely confined in institutions where it was widely believed they were "better off" and "happier" living with "their own kind." It was generally accepted within the therapeutic community that the hospital or residential school was the best setting for the intensive care and treatment many of the disabled need.

These institutions have, by and large, fallen far short of their intended goal. The majority of them have not succeeded in helping those who have entered them to improve their lives. They have, instead, because of overcrowding, poor living conditions, alienating surroundings, inadequate treatment, educational, and recreational programs contributed to the physical, mental, and spiritual deterioration of their inhabitants.

Today, most enlightened professionals in the field agree that even under the best conditions the institutional setting is by its very nature dehumanizing, depersonalizing, and detrimental to individual growth and development. The person confined to an institution does not learn how to become an independent, self-sufficient, self-reliant, productive individual who can take his or her place in society. The institutionalized individual is reduced instead to a state of total childlike dependence on the institution itself, and this "conditioned helplessness," as it is called, which bears no relation to the person's physical disability, prevents him or her from ever leading any kind of life outside the institution.

In recent years, the institution has come to be regarded as the last resort rather than the first choice for the housing and care of the disabled. It is now widely accepted that the disabled are entitled to live in the least restrictive environment available and to lead lives that are as normal and independent as possible. The achievement of this goal involves three separate but related processes: the deinstitutionalization, normalization, and socialization of the disabled.

The term *deinstitutionalization* refers to the process of preventing the unnecessary placement and retention of disabled individuals in institutions and the development of more humane alternatives. The Developmentally Disabled Assistance and Bill of Rights Act of 1971 (PL 94-103) requires that

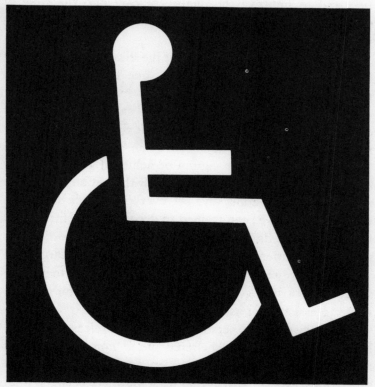

The International Symbol of Access for the Handicapped—designed for display on public buildings, hotels, motels, theaters, restaurants, stores, parking lots, rest rooms, and transportation facilities of all kinds that are fully accessible to wheelchair users and other handicapped persons with limited mobility. (The President's Committee on Employment of the Handicapped)

each state design a plan "to eliminate inappropriate placement in institutions of persons with developmental disabilities, and to improve the quality of care and the state of
surroundings of persons for whom institutional care is appropriate."

Normalization means restoring the disabled individual to
a life of maximum independence, one that is as close to
normal as possible.

Socialization, or "mainstreaming" as it is sometimes
called, is the process of integrating the disabled into regular
society.

Deinstitutionalization cannot be achieved overnight. One
cannot simply unlock the doors of all the nation's hospitals
and residential schools and set everyone inside free. The
disabled who have been trained to depend on the institution
for all their needs have to learn how to think and do for
themselves. Patients have to be prepared for discharge, and
when they are ready to be released, they cannot merely be
set adrift in a strange new environment. Provision must be
made to assist them as they build new lives.

Not every disabled person, whether just released from an
institution or leaving a sheltered life at home for the first
time, will be ready for fully independent living. A broad
range of living alternatives that lie somewhere between total
independence and total dependence need to be made available. These alternative living and treatment facilities should
be located within the community and be considerably
smaller in scale than the traditional institution.

Moreover, the institution itself, although it should now be
viewed only as a last resort, need not be constructed in the

traditional alienating style. The people living in an institution have the right to live in a setting as close to normal as possible. The physical plant can be made to be more like the normal home. Clusters of small homelike buildings each housing a small number of residents could replace the usual mammoth prisonlike compound.

The small group home, housing no more than twenty handicapped individuals, is a more acceptable alternative to the large institution. This type of setting allows for more personal attention, individualized training, and care. It is like the larger institution, however, in that placement in it has usually been considered permanent. The notion that any placement is necessarily permanent is contrary to the philosophy of normalization and needs to be erased.

Hostels, halfway houses, or apartment-living training programs offer the disabled a temporary living arrangement that is meant to ease the transition from sheltered living to independent living. Under this type of arrangement small groups of disabled individuals live in apartment clusters along with teachers who assist them in learning to develop the skills necessary to leading independent lives. These skills include cooking, money management, shopping, and so on. United Cerebral Palsy of New York City has undertaken the development of hostels in each of the four boroughs that it serves. In October of 1973 it leased thirteen apartments on one floor of Tanya Towers on East 13 Street in Manhattan. The facility accommodates sixteen disabled adults, the majority of whom are in transition to more independent living. Similar programs are underway or in the planning stage in the Bronx, Brooklyn, and Staten Island.

When the disabled individual is ready to leave the halfway house, he should be able to choose where and with whom he wishes to live. A number of disabled individuals have chosen communal living. Like a growing number of able-bodied people who opt for this kind of shared living arrangement, many disabled choose it for its financial and personal benefits. Those who need the special care of a nurse or attendant can share the expense under such an arrangement. What distinguishes communal living from the group home or the hostel is the fact that the disabled tenants have chosen where they want to live, with whom they wish to live, and to pay their own way.

The disabled adult who does not wish to live in a communal situation should have the option of living alone. The disabled person who decides to go it alone, however, should still have access to services and care as the need arises.

Dottie Santa Paul, a young woman confined to a wheelchair with a crippling disease, opted for an independent living arrangement after spending twenty-six months in a nursing home for the elderly. "It felt like twenty-six years," she recalls. "I found it very depressing to live with ninety-nine old people, three quarters of whom were senile. . . . I found the rules there very depressing, and I was discouraged from taking any responsibility in the decisions in my life at all. The atmosphere was one of death and awaiting death."

After six discouraging months, trying to find suitable accommodations and attendant care, Dottie was finally able to move into a house with two students who share the responsibility for her personal care and housework. Dottie, who has a degree in social work and is seeking employment in her field, is very happy with this arrangement. "Financially, I make out pretty well, but have learned to live without luxuries," she says. "I get two hundred dollars a month supplemental security income and ninety dollars a month in a rental assistance grant. We share expenses. Independent living is about one hundred and fifty to two hundred dollars a month cheaper than nursing-home living."

These are but a few of the many types of living arrangements that are gradually opening up to the disabled. The one thing that all such housing should have in common is its proximity to the community. Rather than isolating and segregating housing and services away from the community as has been done in the past, the present movement is toward integrating the disabled into community life. This is essential to the ultimate socialization of the disabled.

A number of obstacles still confront the disabled individual who tries to exert his right to choose his own living arrangement. Appropriate alternatives to institutionalization simply do not exist in most communities, and as a result many people released from institutions find themselves worse off than they were before. A 1977 report of the comptroller general to the United States Congress, titled *Returning the Mentally Disabled to the Community: Government Needs to Do More,* based on a study of 164 mentally retarded persons discharged from institutions, found that most ended up in nursing homes where the quality of care was worse than that at the larger institutions; and a majority eventually went back to the institutions because of the lack of community services and facilities.

Another study of five hundred retarded adults released

from institutions in southern California discovered that most were forced to live in segregated ghetto situations in nursing homes and run-down areas where they were once again cut off from community life. The report concluded:

The quality of life in the alternative-care facilities . . . studied is highly variable. . . . For most mentally retarded people in this system . . . the little institutions where they now reside appear to be no better than the large ones from which they came, and some are manifestly worse.

The author of yet another study of this situation cautions:

The philosophy that anything is better than an institutional placement must be seriously questioned, at least on a short-term basis. With sufficient planning, appropriate program implementation, and careful monitoring, community placement can provide excellent opportunities for our handicapped citizens. Without these precautions, hundreds, even thousands of individuals could end up in mini institutions without public attention and resources now available in public institutions.

A major obstacle to the deinstitutionalization of the disabled has always been community opposition to their presence based on fear and prejudice—the "I don't want those funny-looking people in my neighborhood" syndrome. Opposition in some communities is so strong that it has led to violence. In January 1978, a residence planned for the mentally retarded in Greenlawn, Long Island, was burned to the ground by a fire that police believe was set by arsonists. The tactic most often used to prevent groups of the disabled from moving into a residential area is the manipulation of zoning laws. Many communities have laws which require that housing in residential areas be occupied by single families. Groups of unrelated people, such as the disabled in a hostel or communal living situation, are refused housing on the grounds that they do not make up a family in the biological sense. Other zoning ordinances specifically exclude individuals who possess certain "undesirable" characteristics, such as the "insane" or "feeble-minded," from living within residential areas. This kind of community action is blatantly discriminatory and it is used to keep the disabled segregated from community life.

In recent years, a number of lawsuits contesting these prejudicial zoning ordinances have been brought on behalf of disabled persons seeking suitable housing in residential areas. In the case of *The Little Neck Community Association, et al. v. The Working Organization for Retarded Children, et al.,* a New York appellate court upheld a lower court decision in 1976 which stated that a group home for the retarded constituted a family. The judge cited a previous ruling, in the case of *City of White Plains v. Ferrioli* (1974), which stated: "The group home is structured as a single housekeeping unit and is . . . a relatively normal, stable and permanent family unit."

In most communities, opposition to small group residences for the disabled and mentally retarded changes to support once those residences have been established. According to Paul R. Dolan of One-to-One, a non-profit organization that has established fifty homes, "The community residences become a focal point for a lot of vague fears about urban sprawl, property values, sexual assaults and crime. But the barrier is temporary." And Dr. Jennifer L. Howse, Associate Commissioner of Mental Retardation for New York City and Long Island, has said, "I don't know of any case where things didn't stabilize and become positive once the homes were open."

Those disabled who choose to live on their own also face problems in the form of landlords who refuse to rent to them or make alterations in their dwellings for them. In addition, many disabled people do not have sufficient income to pay for decent housing, and they are often forced to live in substandard dwellings in the most run-down, crime-ridden areas, where they become easy prey for criminals. Also, many disabled people are in need of full-time or part-time attendant care, and are unable to afford it if they wish to live independently.

Lack of adequate community-based housing is not the only problem confronting the disabled who wish to lead independent lives. Because the physically or mentally disabled individual has traditionally been viewed as a medical problem rather than a human being with human needs, society at large has adopted a patronizing paternalistic attitude in its dealings with them. The disabled have been generally regarded as childlike, incompetent, and incapable of assuming responsibility for their actions or their lives. As one quadraplegic put it, "Most people equate a serious physical limitation with mental incompetence." Thus members of "normal" society have taken it upon themselves to order and control the lives of the disabled, to dictate where and how they shall live, and how they shall occupy their time.

This assumption of responsibility has often led to a denial of legal rights to the disabled, and the disabled have begun to fight back against a system that has kept them from controlling their own lives. One disabled woman summed up her feelings this way: "I'm tired of able-bodied people sitting behind desks in ivory towers making decisions about my life. Only if you sit in a wheelchair can you tell how people in wheelchairs feel."

When a person reaches adulthood in this country, he or she ordinarily assumes a number of legal rights and responsibilities. Among these are the right to enter contracts and execute legal documents, the right to vote, the right to own and dispose of property, the right to obtain a driver's license, the right to equal protection in the criminal justice system, the right to marry and raise children. These rights are the symbols of adult status. Every adult is considered capable of exercising them, and these rights are protected under the law. Only in extreme cases, when a person is judged in court to be legally incompetent or incapable of making a rational judgment, can these rights be taken away.

Unfortunately it has been the experience of the disabled in the past, particularly the mentally handicapped, that these rights are all too easily taken away. It has been the automatic assumption within society at large that a person in any way mentally impaired is unable to conduct legal affairs. The courts have routinely declared such persons incompetent and placed responsibility for their legal affairs on court-appointed guardians, usually a parent. When this happens, the guardian assumes legal power, and his "ward," no matter what his or her age, is forever after viewed as a child in the eyes of the law, i.e., he or she has no independent legal rights.

The procedure of having a mentally impaired person declared incompetent and having a guardian appointed usually involves a court hearing. In spite of the great importance of the court's decision to the future of the disabled person in question, he or she is rarely allowed the right to be represented by counsel, to present evidence or cross-examine witnesses. In short, he or she is unable to present his or her side of the story or to defend himself or herself properly in a court of law. This is a clear violation of the constitutional rights to due process and equal protection.

An issue closely related to the judgment of competency is the involuntary commitment of mentally handicapped individuals to institutions. This issue has prompted a number of lawsuits on behalf of the mentally retarded in recent years that have argued the violation of due-process rights. In the case of *Kremens v. Bartley,* the federal court in Pennsylvania ruled that state statutes that allowed parents and guardians to place their children in mental-health institutions without the benefit of a court hearing or counsel being provided for the children were unconstitutional. (Nearly three-quarters of the states have similar laws.) Presiding Judge Daniel H. Huyett declared: "The child who faces the possibility of being physically confined for an indeterminate period with all of the ramifications of such confinement clearly has an interest within the contemplation of the liberty and property language of the Fourteenth Amendment." The court went on to note that parents or guardians do not have the right to waive the constitutional rights of their children, because it cannot automatically be presumed that they are acting in the best interests of their children. In order to protect the rights of the child, the court declared that he or she has the right to legal counsel, to be paid for by the state if necessary, that would represent the child in any commitment hearing.

In addition to being a violation of due-process rights, the routine declaration of incompetence and the institutionalization of the mentally handicapped also infringe upon the individual's right to the least drastic means in the limitation of personal freedom.

Ultimately it is the responsibility of each state to come up with alternatives to total legal guardianship and arbitrary permanent confinement in institutions. Several states have experimented successfully with a system of limited guardianship under which the guardian assumes only those responsibilities the mentally retarded person cannot perform for himself. This kind of flexible program which better serves the individual needs of the mentally handicapped is preferable to total guardianship. In addition to this, a system of periodic review of the mentally retarded person's need for guardian services would further insure the protection of his rights. It is possible that a person with a mental handicap can outgrow the need for guardianship, and this must be recognized. The same holds true for the person involuntarily confined to an institution. If the need for confinement is eliminated, then provision must be made to guarantee the individual's release.

One of the most fundamental democratic rights routinely denied the mentally retarded is the right to vote. The right to vote is now guaranteed all American citizens under the Constitution. The Constitution leaves it up to the states, however, to set personal qualifications for exercising the franchise. The states have often used this power to discriminate against certain groups seeking to exercise their right to vote.

Most groups traditionally excluded from the franchise over the years, such as blacks and women, have long enjoyed the right to vote. As a group the mentally retarded have as yet to be so fortunate.

In nearly every state there are outdated statutes that exclude "idiots, morons and the feeble-minded" from the franchise. The lack of a clear definition of what constitutes idiocy or feeble-mindedness has led to the arbitrary disenfranchisement of all retarded individuals regardless of the severity of their impairment.

What is at issue here, once again, is the competence of the individual, i.e., Is she or he able to understand what she or he is doing? It is now generally recognized that the majority of the mentally retarded when properly counseled and instructed are able to make judgments and decisions for themselves. There is no reason, therefore, why a retarded individual who has received adequate instruction in the practice of voting cannot exercise his right to vote in a responsible manner. After all, voting is something we all must *learn* how to do. The mentally retarded person may just need a little more instruction.

If, however, a mentally retarded voter has been declared incompetent and assigned a legal guardian, or he or she is involuntarily confined to an institution, he or she has little chance of exercising his or her right to vote. Protecting the retarded individual's right to vote is another reason for reforming present competency and guardian statutes. No American citizen of voting age who can answer the questions asked of all potential voters when they register to vote should be denied the right to vote. Voting is a social responsibility, and the denial of the franchise to the mentally retarded individual is one more obstacle to normalization of the disabled.

The family unit is a basic component of all societies. The right of a man and a woman to marry and have children is considered fundamental. To deny adults this basic human right is almost unthinkable, yet our nation has a long tradition of just this kind of denial when it comes to individuals who are considered "abnormal" and whose children, it is feared, will also be abnormal.

In the early part of this century the pseudo-science of eugenics—the study of genetic improvement—flourished. The basic idea behind it was that all plant and animal species, including man, could be upgraded through a process of selective breeding. In order to improve the breed, the maximum reproduction of what were considered desirable traits was to be encouraged, while traits that were considered undesirable were to be eliminated.

It is not difficult to see the kinds of abuses that may arise when this type of theory is applied to the human race. Under eugenic theory it was considered good medicine to sterilize those individuals who were deemed to be carriers of undesirable traits. Those usually singled out for sterilization were the "feeble-minded" and the "insane." The eugenic sterilization laws of Nazi Germany, which expanded the candidates for sterilization to include all individuals considered racially or politically "undesirable," were the natural outcome of this movement and the ultimate cause of the scientific community's renunciation of eugenic theory and practice.

In the meantime, however, the acceptance of the theory gave rise to a number of "compulsory sterilization" laws that remain on the books in half our states today. To date, over seventy thousand sterilization operations have been performed, more than half on mentally handicapped persons. About four hundred such operations are still performed each year, in spite of the fact that the modern science of genetics has proven the theoretical basis of eugenics false, and the growing outcry within the legal, medical, and disabled communities against this most outrageous affront to human and civil rights.

As early as 1927, in the case of *Buck v. Bell,* the laws were challenged on the grounds that compulsory sterilization was cruel and unusual punishment. This case reached the Supreme Court, but the court ruled in accordance with the accepted eugenic beliefs of the day. In his now infamous ruling on the case, Justice Oliver Wendell Holmes decreed:

It is better for all the world, if instead of waiting to execute degenerate offspring for crime, or to let them starve for their imbecility, society can prevent those who are manifestly unfit from continuing their kind. The principle that sustains compulsory vaccination is broad enough to cover the cutting of the fallopian tubes. . . . three generations of imbeciles are enough.

In addition to the genetic justifications for sterilizations, a sociological argument was put forth. This argument for sterilization was based on the assumption that certain kinds of people make "unfit" parents. The list of those considered unfit to raise children under this sociological interpretation of eugenic theory grew to include not only the physically and mentally impaired, but the criminal and those considered morally "degenerate" as well. It was the gross violation of human rights, which resulted from this extension of eugenic theory, that finally led to the landmark court case which established procreation as a legal right. In the 1942 case of *Skinner v. Oklahoma,* the Supreme Court held that an Oklahoma statute allowing the involuntary sterilization of criminals was in violation of constitutional rights. The court's opinion stated:

> We are dealing here with legislation which involves one of the basic civil rights of man. Marriage and procreation are fundamental to the very existence and survival of the race. The power to sterilize, if exercised, may have subtle, far-reaching and devastating effects. In evil or reckless hands it can cause races or types which are inimical to the dominate group to wither and disappear. There is no exception for the individual whom the law touches. Any experiment which the state conducts is to his irreparable injury. He is forever deprived of a basic liberty.

In spite of the Supreme Court's recognition of the individual's rights to marry and to procreate, many states still have statutes that call for the denial of these rights. As recently as 1976, the Supreme Court of North Carolina upheld the constitutionality of that state's sterilization laws. In this case, however, the court's ruling called for the protection of the individual's due-process rights, which include notice and a hearing, and prohibited the use of sterilization as a punishment. Other states, however, have not shown the same consideration for the rights of the disabled when it comes to compulsory sterilization.

Clearly any statute that prevents two adults from marrying or allows for persons to be sterilized without their consent, no matter how humanely written or cautiously enforced, is a serious obstacle to the normalization and socialization of the mentally disabled (other people cannot be sterilized without their consent). Not only do such laws violate the individual's rights to due process, least drastic means, equal protection, and freedom from cruel and unusual punishment, they further stigmatize and isolate the mentally retarded from the rest of society. Furthermore, compulsory-sterilization statutes call for those in control of the law to play God with the lives of the mentally disabled. Such laws are based on the assumption that the mentally impaired are less than human and incapable of controlling their own destinies.

There is no reason for the continued physical violation of the mentally disabled through the barbaric custom of compulsory sterilization. It is now known that only a very few mental disorders are genetically transmitted. (It is interesting to note that at least 80 percent of all mentally impaired individuals are born of "normal" parents. So much for eugenic theory!) It is also generally accepted by experts on mental disorders that even the most severely retarded individual is capable of intellectual development and personal growth. Most mentally retarded individuals, therefore, are as capable in the area of child-rearing as the normal person, with the aid of supporting services where a need is indicated. For those few who are unable to cope with the responsibilities involved in parenthood, there are other alternatives less drastic than compulsory sterilization. Birth-control devices to prevent unwanted pregnancies from occurring, and abortion and adoption, are certainly preferable to a procedure so serious and irrevocable as sterilization. Of course, sterilization should be made available to the mentally handicapped individual who desires it, but it must be a voluntary, informed, noncoerced decision. It should never be forced upon anyone unknowingly or unwillingly.

Other serious obstacles to the normalization of the physically and mentally disabled that deserve attention are to be found in the areas of insurance coverage and criminal justice. The disabled are often considered "bad risks" by insurance companies, and they are routinely refused coverage. Health insurance and automobile insurance are an essential part of normal life in our society. A great many disabled consumers are prevented from obtaining coverage, however, because of discriminatory practices on the part of insurers.

The disabled individual who faces criminal prosecution must also deal with discrimination. It is a fact that 10 percent of the prison population in this country is mentally retarded (in some areas the figure runs as high as 24 percent). This is compared to a 3 percent incidence in the general population. The reason for such a disproportionate representation of the mentally impaired in prison is not a result of their inherent "criminal nature" as some people still believe. It is, rather, the result of inadequacies in our criminal-justice system's treatment of the mentally disabled.

In many cases the court fails adequately to inform the mentally retarded defendant of his or her rights and the nature of the criminal proceeding in which he or she is involved because the defendant's impaired mental capacity goes undetected. Special care must be taken with the mentally retarded individual accused of a criminal act so that his or her rights to due process and equal protection are not violated. Similar consideration is needed for the hearing-impaired individual in certain judicial proceedings. If one cannot hear what is being said in the courtroom, one cannot properly present one's case. The hearing-impaired have been lobbying for quite some time at the state level for laws that would require the presence of a qualified interpreter at all such proceedings.

The disabled have also been denied full participation in another part of our legal system—the jury. Disabled potential jurors, particularly those who are blind, are regularly judged "noncompetent" and excluded from jury service. This practice continues in spite of the fact that there are a great number of blind lawyers, prosecutors, and judges in United States courts. (Even the goddess of justice is portrayed with a blindfold, symbolizing her impartiality in judging the evidence placed upon her scale.)

*   *   *

The biggest problem facing the disabled in the United States today is the same one they have been forced to confront since the dawn of history—isolation, exclusion, segregation. It has many names, but they all mean the same thing to the disabled.

Recent legislation, court decrees, and changing attitudes within the medical community appear to be bringing to an end the era of the disabled individual's status as outcast, freak, second-class citizen. Most important of all, the disabled are now taking responsibility for the direction of their own lives, and they have begun to attract widespread public support for their cause. At the White House Conference on Handicapped Individuals held in May 1977, President Jimmy Carter pledged the support of his administration to the protection of the rights of the handicapped and called for an end to "discrimination against the handicapped in America."

That is only the beginning. Undoing years of bad feeling, fear, and prejudice will not be easy, but if we can remember how much we as Americans prize our independence, our right to choose how we conduct our lives, and our devotion to the democratic principles of freedom and equality, then the full participation in our society of a newly liberated class of disabled individuals should be possible in the near future.

SELECTED BIBLIOGRAPHY

DOCUMENTS AND BOOKS

Arthur, Julietta K. *Employment for the Handicapped.* New York: Abingdon Press, 1967.

Bensberg, Gerard J., and Carolyn Rude, eds., *Advocacy Systems for the Disabled.* Texas Tech University Press, 1976.

Educational Facilities Laboratories and the National Endowment for the Arts. *Arts and the Handicapped, An Issue of Access.* New York, 1975.

Educational Facilities Laboratories. *One Out of Ten: School Planning for the Handicapped.* New York, 1974.

Haskins, James. *Who Are the Handicapped?* Garden City: Doubleday & Company, 1978.

Jaffe, A. J., Lincoln H. Day, and Walter Adams. *Disabled Workers in the Labor Market.* Somerset, N.J.: Bedminster Press, 1964.

Katz, Alfred, D.S.W. *Parents of the Handicapped.* Springfield, Illinois: Charles C. Thomas, Publisher, 1961.

Klimet, Stephan A. *Into the Mainstream: A Syllabus for a Barrier-Free Environment.* The American Institute of Architects, 1975.

Kvaraceus, William C., and Nelson Hayes. *If Your Child Is Handicapped.* Boston: Porter Sargent, 1969.

Laurie, Gini. *Housing and Home Service for the Disabled.* New York: Harper & Row, 1977.

Selected Bibliography

Mann, Philip H., ed. *Shared Responsibility for Handicapped Students, Advocacy and Programming.* Miami: University of Miami Training and Assistance Center, 1976.

Mental Health Law Project. *Basic Rights of the Mentally Handicapped.* Washington, D.C., 1973.

Rivera, Geraldo. *Willowbrook: A Report on How It Is and Why It Doesn't Have to Be That Way.* New York: Random House, 1972.

Scott, Rachel. *Muscle and Blood.* New York: E. P. Dutton & Co., 1974.

ARTICLES

The New York Times

"Agency Lists But Does Not Notify Workers Exposed to Carcinogens." April 25, 1977.

Aiello, Barbara. "Keeping the Multiple Handicapped in Regular Classes." April 30, 1978.

———. "2 Colleges Open Their Doors to the Retarded." January 8, 1978.

———. "Buildings Work for the Blind." December 3, 1976.

Brody, Jane E. "Specialists Look to Preventive Medicine to Improve the Nation's Health." May 30, 1978.

Burnham, David. "U. S. Study Finds One in 4 Workers Exposed to Hazards." October 3, 1977.

Cerra, Frances. "Residences for the Retarded Earn Wider Acceptance." February 14, 1979.

Fedo, Michael W. "Rehabilitation is Good Business." August 6, 1978.

Fiske, Edward B. "Special Education Is Now a Matter of Civil Rights." April 25, 1976.

136

Flint, Jerry. "Handicapped No Longer Act Like It." October 2, 1977.

Goldberger, Paul. "Library for Blind an Architectural Triumph." August 9, 1978.

————. "Handicapped Campaign for Rights to Mobility, Jobs and Education." December 13, 1976.

Hechinger, Fred M. "Bringing the Handicapped Into the Mainstream." April 25, 1976.

Hicks, Nancy. "Califano Signs Regulations to Ban Discrimination Against Disabled." April 29, 1977.

————. "Equity for Disabled Likely to Be Costly." May 1, 1977.

Hill, Gladwin. "Factory Noise is Union's Target." May 2, 1976.

Holsendolph, Ernest. "Blind Protesters Gather in Capitol to Assail Aviation Rules on Canes." July 6, 1978.

Houts, Paul L. "I.Q. Tests Once Again Disturb Educators." May 1, 1977.

Maeroff, Gene I. "Teachers Weigh Limit on Number of Handicapped Pupils per Class." August 19, 1976.

McElheny, Victor K. "Print-to-Speech Devices Are Expected to Aid the Blind." January 14, 1976.

Milofsky, David. "Schooling the Kids No One Wants." January 2, 1977.

————. "Polio Victim with Incentive Pays Price for His Success." December 27, 1977.

Reif, Rita. "Home Design Is Life and Death for Disabled." February 5, 1976.

Rosenbaum, David E. "Huge Federal Disability Program Faces Inequities, Fund Woes, Suits." July 27, 1977.

Russell, John. "At Met Museum, A Show for the Blind." August 7, 1977.

Schultz, Terri. "The Handicapped, A Minority Demanding its

137

Rights." February 13, 1977.

Shenker, Israel. "Art Museum Exhibit Gives Blind 'Feel' of Art." August 4, 1977.

―――. "Talents of Handicapped Children Being Developed in Connecticut." September 26, 1976.

Tolchin, Martin. "Intervention by Courts Arouses Deepening Disputes." April 24, 1977.

Wicker, Tom. "The Low-Floor Bus." March 15, 1977.

OTHER ARTICLES

Clark, Matt. "Electronic Eyes." *Newsweek,* May 24, 1976.

"Disability Insurance." *New York Magazine,* April 26, 1976.

"Ears to Hearings." *National Observer,* September 18, 1976.

"Freedom in a Wheelchair." *Time,* June 21, 1976.

"Helping the Disabled Pay Their Way." *International Management,* June 1975.

Hillman, Bruce P. "You Gave Us Your Dimes. . . ." *Newsweek,* November 1, 1976.

Kellog, Mary Alice, and Henry McGee. "The Next Minority." *Newsweek,* December 20, 1976.

Kriegel, Leonard. "Uncle Tom and Tiny Tim: Some Reflections on the Cripple as Negro." *The American Scholar,* Summer 1964, Vol. 38, No. 3.

Kukuk, Jack W., and James A. Sjolund. "Arts for the Handicapped: A National Direction." *National Elementary Principal,* Vol. 55, No. 3, January/February 1976.

Laski, Frank. "Civil Rights Victories for the Handicapped." Parts I and II. *Social Rehabilitation Record,* May and June 1974.

Shriver, Eunice Kennedy. "Physical Education: Shortest Road to Success for the Handicapped." *Science and*

Children Magazine, March 1976.

Wolfe, Joe. "Disability Is No Handicap for du Pont." *The Alliance Review,* Winter 1973–74.

———. "You Can't Get There from Here." *Journal of American Insurance,* Spring 1974.

Zerface, W. A. "Hire the Handicapped Librarian!" *Wilson Library Bulletin,* Vol. 51, No. 8, April 1977.

GOVERNMENT DOCUMENTS

Department of Health, Education, and Welfare

Child Advocacy. Office of Child Development, Children's Bureau. 1973.

Education of the Handicapped and a Bill of Rights for the Handicapped. Reprinted from *American Education,* July 1976. Office of Education.

First Report of the Architectural and Transportation Barriers Compliance Board to the Congress of the United States. November 1974.

Freedom of Choice, Report to the Congress on Housing Needs of Handicapped Individuals. Architectural and Transportation Barriers Compliance Board. October 1975.

Improving Services to Handicapped Children. The Rand Corporation. 1974.

Mental Retardation: The Known and the Unknown. President's Committee on Mental Retardation. February 1, 1975.

Mental Retardation and the Law. January 1977.

The Problem of Mental Retardation. Office of Handicapped Individuals. June 1975.

Report to the President: Century of Decision. President's Committee on Mental Retardation. March 1976.

Selected Bibliography

The Unfinished Revolution: Education for the Handicapped. National Advisory Committee on the Handicapped. Annual Report, 1976.

OTHER GOVERNMENT DOCUMENTS

Affirmative Action to Employ Handicapped People. President's Committee on Employment of the Handicapped, 1976.

Day on Wheels. General Services Administration, Public Buildings Service, January 1975.

A Handbook on the Legal Rights of Handicapped People. President's Committee on Employment of the Handicapped.

Hiring the Handicapped: Facts and Myths. President's Committee on Employment of the Handicapped.

Pollution and Your Health. Office of Public Affairs, United States Environmental Protection Agency, May 1976.

Report to the Congress: Further Action Needed to Make All Public Buildings Accessible to the Physically Handicapped. The Comptroller General of the United States, July 15, 1975.

Report to the Congress: Summary of a Report—Returning the Mentally Disabled to the Community: Government Needs to Do More. The Comptroller General of the United States, January 7, 1977.

Respond To: Workers With Epilepsy. President's Committee on Employment of the Handicapped.

PAMPHLETS

A Bill of Rights for the Handicapped. United Cerebral Palsy Associations, Inc., 1973.

Declaration on the Rights of Disabled Persons. United Nations

Selected Bibliography

General Assembly Resolution, adopted 9 December 1975.

Emerson, Thomas I. *The Bill of Rights Today.* Public Affairs Pamphlet, No. 489, 1973.

Gailis, Ann, and Keith M. Susman. *Abroad in the Land: Legal Strategies to Effectuate the Rights of the Physically Disabled.* Reprinted from *The Georgetown Law Journal,* Volume 61, Number 6, July 1973.

Hiring Handicapped People. National Association of Manufacturers.

Information Sheet on Federal Affirmative Action for the Disabled. Disability Rights Center, Inc., March 1977.

Ogg, Elizabeth. *Securing the Legal Rights of Retarded Persons.* Public Affairs Pamphlet, No. 492, June 1975.

Wright, Beatrice A., Ph. D. *Disabling Myths About Disability.* Address Delivered at the 1961 Annual Convention of the National Easter Seal Society for Crippled Children and Adults.

PERIODICALS AND NEWSLETTERS

Amicus. National Center for Law and the Handicapped. Vol. 1, Nos. 1, 2, 3, 4, 5, 6, 1975–76; Vol. 2, Nos. 1, 2, 3, 4, 5, 6, 1976–77; Vol. 3, Nos. 1, 2, 3, 4, 1978.

Polling. United Cerebral Palsy of New York City, Inc. Vol. 1, No. 1, May 1974; Vol 2, No. 1, March 1976; Vol. 2, No. 4, Fall 1976; Vol. 3, No. 1, Spring 1977.

Report. National Center for a Barrier Free Environment. Vol. 2, Nos. 1, 2, 3, 4, 5, 6.

INDEX

Index

ABOUT THE AUTHORS

JAMES HASKINS is presently Associate Professor in the Department of English at the University of Florida. He has taught in elementary and junior high schools, the New School for Social Research, the State University College at New Paltz, New York, Staten Island Community College, and Indiana University-Purdue University at Indianapolis. He is also an educational consultant, a book reviewer, and the author of more than thirty published books, including *A New Kind of Joy: The Story of the Special Olympics, Who Are the Handicapped?,* and *The Creoles of Color of New Orleans.* Born in Alabama, Mr. Haskins now commutes to Gainesville, Florida, from New York City, where he makes his permanent home.

J M STIFLE is a free-lance writer who lives in New York City. She has written for children's television and is the author of *The Truth or Baloney Book About Animals.*